GETTING THE
GOSPELS

GETTING THE GOSPELS

Understanding the New Testament

Accounts of Jesus' Life

Steven L. Bridge

© 2004 by Steven L. Bridge

Hendrickson Publishers, Inc.
P. O. Box 3473
Peabody, Massachusetts 01961-3473

ISBN 1-56563-943-X

Printed in the United States of America

Second Printing — February 2005

NIHIL OBSTAT
Monsignor Charles M. Murphy, STD, *Censor Deputatus*

IMPRIMATUR
Most Reverend Richard J. Malone, ThD, *Bishop of Portland*

July 9, 2004

The *nihil obstat* and *imprimatur* are official declarations that a book or pamphlet is free of doctrinal or moral error. No implication is contained therein that those who have granted the *nihil obstat* and *imprimatur* agree with the contents, opinions, or statements expressed.

Library of Congress Cataloging-in-Publication Data

Bridge, Steven L.
    Getting the Gospels : understanding the New Testament accounts of Jesus' life / Steven L. Bridge.
        p. cm.
    Includes bibliographical references and index.
    ISBN 1-56563-943-X (alk. paper)
    1. Bible. N.T. Gospels—Criticism, interpretation, etc. I. Title.
BS2555.52.B75 2004
226'.06—dc22
                                                            2004016509

To Leonard and Gerrie Bridge,
the greatest teachers I've ever had,

and

To Kamal, Heather, Erica, and Emily Bridge,
for their patience and encouragement throughout this project.

Table of Contents

SECTION III—JESUS' PASSION, DEATH, AND RESURRECTION

List of Figures

Preface

*I*n order to make this book accessible to a wide audience, I have deliberately downplayed some of the more technical aspects of biblical studies, including scholarly jargon, critical methodology, Greek and Hebrew vocabulary, and direct engagement with the secondary literature. Although facets of these elements have certainly influenced the conclusions drawn here, for the sake of brevity and lucidity I have endeavored to keep them largely out of view. At the back of this book I have provided a list of recommended resources for those readers who are interested in examining the gospels in greater depth or breadth. Included in that list is a recently published work of my own, a more sophisticated study of the premises behind Luke 17:37 ("Where the body is, there the eagles will be gathered together").

I have also ventured to write this book in an ecumenical spirit. For this reason, all of the biblical quotations that appear here have been drawn from one of three translations: the (traditionally Catholic) New American Bible, the (traditionally Protestant) Revised Standard Version, and the (traditionally Jewish) *Tanakh: The Holy Scriptures: The New JPS Translation according to the Traditional Hebrew Text*. My goal is not to confuse my audience, but to impress upon us all the relevance of this information for anyone who wants to understand Jesus as the evangelists did.

DANVILLE LIBRARY
Contra Costa County Library
400 Front St.
Danville, CA 94526
(925) 837-4889

Customer ID: 21901012135319

Title: Getting the Gospels : understanding the
New Testament accounts of Jesus' life /
ID: 31901037536382
Due: 22 Jul 2018
Circulation system messages:
Item checked out.

Total Items: 1
7/1/2018 2:10 PM

Renew Online or by Phone
ccclib.org
1-800-984-4636

Have a great day!

Acknowledgments

I owe a tremendous debt of gratitude to those individuals who helped make this book a reality. First and foremost, I'd like to thank Shirley Decker-Lucke, Dawn C. Harrell, and the other editors at Hendrickson Publishers who assisted in this project. Because much of the content here has been developed and refined in the context of the classroom, I am also extremely grateful for the teaching positions extended to me over the years at Hackett Catholic Central (Kalamazoo, Mich.), Mount Mary College (Milwaukee, Wis.), Marquette University (Milwaukee, Wis.), and St. Joseph's College (Standish, Maine). The chain of events that brought this work into being may never have come about without the support of St. Joseph's College in general, and its Vice President for Academic Affairs, Daniel Sheridan, in particular. I owe perhaps the greatest debt of gratitude to my wife, Kamal. She and Melissa Ransom (a former student of mine) read through earlier drafts of my manuscript and offered some helpful suggestions. More importantly, Kamal shouldered many of the additional responsibilities created by my absence as I worked on this book. She has repeatedly proven herself to be my "suitable helpmate," and in that spirit I consider this to be the product of our collaborative effort. I thank God for her and for the blessing this project has been for me.

As an expression of my gratitude, I have agreed to commit the majority of my royalties generated from this book to humanitarian projects benefiting the poorest of the poor. On several occasions, I have had the privilege of working among such people in Haiti and elsewhere. I have come to discover that the things I tend to take for granted (food, clothing, shelter, clean water, medicine, education, and employment) are, for many people throughout the world, rare commodities. In some small way, I'd like to make these necessities a little more prevalent. On behalf of the beneficiaries, I thank you, the reader, for enabling this to happen. *Soli Deo Gloria.* To God alone be the glory.

Steven L. Bridge

Abbreviations

GENERAL

BCE	Before the Common Era
ca.	circa
CE	Common Era
cf.	*confer*, compare
ch(s).	chapter(s)
lit.	literally
Midr.	*Midrash*
NAB	New American Bible
NIV	New International Version
NJPS	*Tanakh: The Holy Scriptures: The New JPS Translation according to the Traditional Hebrew Text*
NT	New Testament
OT	Old Testament
RSV	Revised Standard Version
v(v).	verse(s)
vol(s).	volume(s)

HEBREW BIBLE / OLD TESTAMENT

Gen	Genesis
Exod	Exodus
Lev	Leviticus
Num	Numbers
Deut	Deuteronomy
Josh	Joshua
Judg	Judges
1–2 Sam	1–2 Samuel
1–2 Kgs	1–2 Kings

1–2 Chr	1–2 Chronicles
Neh	Nehemiah
Ps	Psalms
Eccl	Ecclesiastes
Isa	Isaiah
Jer	Jeremiah
Ezek	Ezekiel
Dan	Daniel
Hos	Hosea
Mic	Micah
Hab	Habakkuk
Mal	Malachi

APOCRYPHA

1–2 Macc	1–2 Maccabees
Tob	Tobit

NEW TESTAMENT

Matt	Matthew
Rom	Romans
1–2 Cor	1–2 Corinthians
Phil	Philippians
Heb	Hebrews
Rev	Revelation

MISHNAH

m.	tractate of the Mishnah
Ker.	*Keritot*
Pesah.	*Pesahim*
Seb.	*Shevi'it*

JOSEPHUS

Ag. Ap.	*Against Apion*
Ant.	*Jewish Antiquities*
J. W.	*Jewish War*

OTHER ANCIENT WRITERS

Philo
    Virt.   *On the Virtues*
Pliny the Elder
    Nat.   *Natural History*
Tacitus
    Ann.   *The Annals of Imperial Rome*

Introduction

From James Cameron to Jesus Christ

*O*n March 23, 1998, the motion picture industry's most re-nowned celebrities gathered together in Los Angeles for the presentation of *The 70th Annual Academy Awards.* Shrine Auditorium, the site of the black-tie extravaganza, was lavishly awash in all of the elegance and glamour one would expect from Hollywood's biggest night. As the stars arrived and made their way through throngs of fans, press reporters, and security personnel, the excitement grew in anticipation of the evening's outcomes. Dominating the buzz was *Titanic,* the historically based film that had cost 20th Century Fox/ Paramount an unprecedented $200 million to produce. The studio's financial gamble had already netted its payoff. In the thirteen weeks since its debut, *Titanic* had earned some $471.4 million in domestic box office receipts and another $693.3 million in foreign sales to displace *Star Wars* as the top-grossing movie of all time.

What remained to be seen was whether *Titanic* could also capture the industry's highest critical honor—the Oscar. Actually, the question was not *whether* the film would win an Oscar, but rather, *how many* Oscars *Titanic* would claim. With its fourteen Academy Award nominations (tying the record set by *All about Eve* in 1950), this dramatic epic was on the verge of making Hollywood history.

In contrast to its namesake, *Titanic* sailed through the evening unimpeded. The film swept nearly all of the categories for which it had been nominated. By the time James Cameron was called to the stage to receive his Oscar for Best Director, *Titanic* had collected nine Academy Awards. Cameron's made ten. (It would eventually go on to take Best Picture, tying *Ben-Hur's* record for the most Oscars ever.)

Understandably, Cameron was exuberant. Before an estimated television audience of eighty-seven million viewers, he ascended the stage, accepted his golden statuette, and stepped to the podium to say a few words. It was during the latter part of his speech that Cameron proceeded to make his own indelible mark in the annals of history. After expressing his gratitude to those directly associated with the film, his sentiments turned to his parents. He addressed these words to them:

> Mom, Dad, there's no way that I can express to you what I'm feeling right now—my heart is full to bursting—except to say, "I'm king of the world! Whoo-whoo!!"[1]

In the days, weeks, and months to follow, the press and various members of the Academy harshly criticized Cameron for his apparent self-adulation. Editorials and opinion columns in newspapers nationwide branded his speech "immodest,"[2] "conceited,"[3] and "embarrassingly jerklike."[4] One writer described Cameron's statement as "hubris to the max,"[5] and another claimed that it "explains why many in the industry find him an insufferable egomaniacal bore."[6] Perhaps the harshest criticism of Cameron's words appeared in *The New York Times*. There, they were said to have "set a standard for orgiastic self-congratulation."[7] It seems Cameron's terse quip would prove to be the proverbial iceberg in his otherwise spectacular voyage with *Titanic*.

On the face of it, the expression, "I'm king of the world," conveys a brazen claim to sovereign authority. One might expect it from Alexander the Great, Genghis Khan, or Napoleon. It conjures up notions of power, dominion, and domination. Such is its literal interpretation. And in the wake of The 70th Annual Academy Awards, such was its ubiquitous *mis*interpretation.

What many of Cameron's critics failed to consider was that the honored director had used a borrowed line. His words originated not from some self-impressed conqueror, but from Jack Dawson, *Titanic's* affable young hero (played by Leonardo DiCaprio).

According to the story, Jack is a free-spirited artist whose dreams appear capable of carrying him further than his financial resources.

In the opening scenes of the film, he wins a poker game in a dockside saloon when his full-house narrowly edges out two-pair. His windfall includes two tickets for passage aboard the celebrated luxury liner. *Titanic* is bound for America, and with the turn of a card, Jack and his pal Fabrizio now join a group of select passengers privileged enough to experience its maiden voyage.

Once out of port, Jack and Fabrizio make their way to the vessel's bow. There, the endless blue horizon stretches out before them. As *Titanic* plies resolutely through the water, Jack looks down and spies a pod of dolphins. The sleek creatures race alongside the mammoth prow, occasionally breaching the surface with their powerful, graceful leaps. Jack watches them excitedly for several moments. He then ascends the guardrail, spreads his arms, throws back his head, and, overcome with emotion, proclaims, "I'm king of the world! Whoo-whoo!!"

The moment is cinematically charged, and few moviegoers are offended when DiCaprio delivers this line. His exclamation is not intended to communicate a message of monarchical aspiration. Rather, *it conveys the character's inexpressible joy in the face of such rare good fortune.*

No doubt it was this context that James Cameron had in mind when he made his own declaration. As the Director (and Editor) of the film, Cameron would have been intimately familiar with all of its details. He would have known every line by heart. His use of this particular quotation was hardly coincidental. Cameron repeated it because he wanted to capture precisely those sentiments conveyed by Jack. (In fact, when he delivered his speech, Cameron not only adopted Jack's words, he mimicked Jack's posture as well.) Like Jack, Cameron intended to communicate his rush of happiness in the face of such improbable success. The only problem was that Cameron had assumed that his audience had all seen the movie and would be able to make this association. Unfortunately, Cameron's words were completely misconstrued by those who failed to consider their premise.

Webster's Dictionary defines a "premise" as "a proposition [previously] supposed as a basis of inference; something assumed or taken for granted; [a] presupposition." To break it down, a premise can be thought of as the story behind the story. Cameron's personal saga is a particularly apt example of why premises matter. In this case, those who neglected to account for the story behind Cameron's words assigned to them a nearly *opposite* meaning. They missed his point entirely.

What does any of this have to do with the interpretation of the gospels? Quite a bit, as it turns out. The Bible is replete with analogous examples. At first glance, many passages may seem to have rather obvious meanings. However, once their historical premises are taken into consideration, their messages can change dramatically. One such instance occurs in the account of Jesus' passion as it is found in the gospels of Matthew and Mark. A brief recap of Mark 14–15//Matthew 26–27 may help to set the stage.

According to the evangelists, Jesus was betrayed by Judas, his disciple, in the garden of Gethsemane. This event took place at night, shortly following their Passover meal together. Jesus was arrested and taken before the Sanhedrin, a judiciary council of chief priests and elders, where he was pronounced guilty of blasphemy because of his claim to be the Son of God. Since the Jewish law considered blasphemy to be a capital crime (so Lev 24:10–16), Jesus was sentenced to death. The Sanhedrin had been granted some autonomous power, but Roman law prohibited it from carrying out capital punishment. Therefore, the Jewish leaders bound Jesus and delivered him to Pilate, the Roman governor, so that he might be executed. Fearing a riot from the large and boisterous crowd, Pilate capitulated and ordered that Jesus be scourged and crucified. Roman soldiers led Jesus to a place called Golgotha, where he was crucified between two thieves. As he was hanging on the cross, the soldiers cast lots for Jesus' garments while the onlookers wagged their heads and derided him. Even those crucified beside him taunted him openly: "He trusted in God; let him deliver him now if he wants him!" For some three hours, darkness covered the land. Then, just before he expired, Jesus cried out in a loud voice, "My God, my God, why have you forsaken me?" (Matt 27:46//Mark 15:34 NAB).

Biblical commentators variously describe Jesus' cry as conveying "the profound horror,"[8] "the total desolation,"[9] and "the unmitigated bitterness"[10] of Jesus' experience. As such, Jesus' final utterance poses a serious challenge to some of the most fundamental tenets of Christianity. Taken literally, it seems to suggest that either (a) Jesus lost his faith in God, or (b) God deserted Jesus. Of course, either interpretation is scandalous. In response, Christian thinkers down through the ages have performed metaphysical gymnastics in order to soften the apparent meaning of Jesus' words.

It has been reasoned, for instance, that Jesus finally succumbed to the emotional, physical, and psychological stress of his suffering, and that his "cry of dereliction" was simply a natural human response to a life-threatening situation. While this may be true, it fails to consider Jesus' unusual courage in the face of other life-threatening situations (see, e.g., Mark 4:35–41//Matt 8:23–27, where Jesus stills the storm). It also runs contrary to Jesus' message about trusting God always—even in the face of extreme persecution (e.g., Mark 13:9–13//Matt 24:9–13). In light of this evidence, one must question whether these gospels were really intent on presenting a Jesus who failed to practice what he preached. This hardly seems possible.

The alternative is to assert that Jesus retained his faith to the end, but that, for some reason, God deserted him. God's absence has been variously explained. Perhaps God was *testing* Jesus. If this were the case, however, it would require God to reverse roles with Satan, who previously tested Jesus in Mark 1:12–13//Matt 4:1–11. Or perhaps Jesus so embodied the sin of the world that God could not be present at that moment. But what of God's omnipotence and omnipresence? And what of Jesus' divinity? These characteristics are repeatedly affirmed throughout the gospels. At any rate, God's supposed abandonment runs contrary to the portrayal of his steadfast compassion and dependability. It seems rather incredulous that these gospels would even attempt to advocate faith in a God who would turn his back on his own beloved Son during his greatest moment of need.

The apparent dilemma and subsequent confusion stem from a failure to recognize that Jesus' utterance, like James Cameron's, is a *borrowed line.* To interpret it without consideration of its background is to essentially *misinterpret* it. In fact, "My God, my God, why have you abandoned me?" is the first line of Psalm 22. In the next stanza, the psalmist provides an even fuller expression of his frustration:

> Why so far from my call for help, from my cries of anguish? My God, I call by day, but you do not answer; by night, but I have no relief. (Ps 22:1–2 NAB)

As he continues, however, the psalmist changes his tenor. He affirms God's faithfulness as it has been demonstrated throughout Israel's history:

Yet you are enthroned as the Holy One; you are the glory of Israel. In you our ancestors trusted; they trusted and you rescued them. To you they cried out and they escaped; in you they trusted and were not disappointed. (Ps 22:4–6 NAB)

The psalmist then offers a detailed description of his own situation—a situation that bears striking similarity to Jesus':

But I am a worm, hardly human, scorned by everyone, despised by the people. All who see me mock me; they curl their lips and jeer; they shake their heads at me: "You relied on the LORD—let him deliver you; if he loves you, let him rescue you." . . . Like water, my life drains away; all my bones grow soft. My heart has become like wax, it melts away within me. As dry as a potsherd is my throat; my tongue sticks to my palate; you lay me in the dust of death. Many dogs surround me; a pack of evildoers closes in on me. So wasted are my hands and feet that I can count all my bones. They stare at me and gloat; they divide my garments among them; for my clothing they cast lots. (Ps 22:6–8, 14–18 NAB)

Next, the psalmist implores God to rescue him:

But you, LORD, do not stay far off; my strength, come quickly to help me. Deliver me from the sword, my forlorn life from the teeth of the dog. Save me from the lion's mouth, my poor life from the horns of wild bulls. (Ps 22:20–22 NAB)

The psalmist finally concludes his petition by affirming his confidence in God:

Then I will proclaim your name to the assembly; in the community I will praise you: "You who fear the LORD, give praise! All descendants of Jacob, give honor; show reverence, all descendants of Israel! For God has not spurned or disdained the misery of this poor wretch, did not turn away from me, but heard me when I cried out. . . . All who sleep in the earth will bow low before God; all who have gone down into the dust will kneel in homage. And I will live for the LORD; my descendants will serve you. The generation to come will be told of the Lord, that they may proclaim to a people yet unborn the deliverance you have brought. (Ps 22:22–24, 29–31 NAB)

Clearly, the overall outlook of Psalm 22 is not despairing, but hopeful. Its author finds himself in a dire situation. He is thirsty and near death. His enemies have surrounded him. They shake their heads, divide up his possessions, and ridicule his faith in God. Yet despite all this, the psalmist asserts his confidence in God's ability to save him. He even goes so far as to anticipate telling subsequent generations about his deliverance!

Jesus was an observant Jew and teacher (rabbi) of the Jewish tradition. He would have been intimately familiar with the Psalms, as would have his earliest followers. That Jesus quotes the opening to this particular psalm can hardly be judged coincidence. It resonates precisely with his situation. He, too, is scorned and mocked; he is thirsty and physically languishing; his enemies cast lots for his garments and ridicule his reliance on God. In short, Jesus' very *posture* reflects that of the psalmist.

It stands to reason that Jesus' adoption of both the words and the posture of Psalm 22 indicates his intention to convey its message as well. Therefore, Jesus' departing exclamation does not signal a momentary lapse of faith or reveal some divine dissociation. Rather, Jesus cites Psalm 22 to demonstrate his unshakable trust in God's ability to save—despite all of the appearances to the contrary. In light of its premise, the *meaning* of Jesus' statement is precisely the *opposite* of its literal interpretation. It is not despair that Jesus expresses, but faith.

That this message eludes those unaware of its origin is not surprising. It presupposes a familiarity with the Jewish Scriptures. This prerequisite is almost certainly why the gospel of Luke, which was written to a largely Gentile audience, records Jesus as quoting an entirely different psalm: "Father, into your hands I commend my spirit!" (Luke 23:46 NAB, see Ps 31:5). The gospel of John likewise records different words. There, Jesus merely exclaims, "It is finished!" (John 19:30 NAB). No doubt the authors of these gospels sought to avoid the confusion Jesus' cry would have tended to create among their non-Jewish readers.

Of course, the implication that early Christian writers may have taken such liberties with Jesus' words raises modern questions of integrity and historical accuracy. In our present society, it would be considered unethical for a reporter or an editor to similarly alter a quotation destined for publication. In extreme cases, such behavior can be deemed libelous and legally prosecuted. However, even today there are situations that arise in which the interpretation of a message is preferable to its literal rendering.

Imagine, for example, an American observer backstage in the moments before the curtain rises on an Italian opera. The American asks a nearby translator to tell a performer to "Break a leg!" Being from Italy, the singer wouldn't know the intent behind this expression. Furthermore, a literal translation would wind up conveying the very opposite meaning the observer sought to express. The performer would assume the American intended her harm rather than luck! Therefore, the translator would be entirely justified in rewording the observer's message for the sake of clarity. To transmit it otherwise would be irresponsible. Evidently, Luke and John would have agreed.

The quotations above illustrate the impact that assumptions can have on interpretation and meaning. It's not that the New Testament (NT) contains some sort of secret mystery whose enigmatic truths are revealed only to those worthy enough to receive them (any more than Cameron's acceptance speech or the "Break a leg!" idiom do). Rather, like any other form of communication, the gospels are the products of very specific times and places. Their authors naturally took their own contemporary social, political, cultural, and religious paradigms for granted, and they assumed that their audiences would, too. Admittedly, that puts modern readers of the Bible at a disadvantage. Obviously, the ancients' frames of references are no longer our own. Therefore it becomes incumbent upon *us* to learn and adopt *their* worldviews. As inconvenient as this may seem, the payoffs are well worth it. For it is only in light of their historical premises that readers of the gospels can truly grasp the portrayals of Jesus as their authors originally intended.

The following chapters will examine some of these stories behind the stories. The examples I have selected are by no means exhaustive. Rather, I have sought to present a broad and balanced sampling of each of the gospels as they span Jesus' entire career. My hope is that these forays into the biblical text will help bring it to life, so that the reader might discover just how rich these documents are, and how rewarding their study can be!

I

The Early Years

For the sake of convenience, I have divided this book into three sections—The Early Years; Jesus' Public Ministry; and Jesus' Passion, Death, and Resurrection. In this first section, we will concentrate on those aspects of Jesus' life that serve to introduce him and to set the stage for his public ministry. In chapter 1, we'll decipher some of the messages conveyed by Jesus' genealogy. In chapter 2, we'll unravel the nativity stories to reveal, not one, but two very different accounts of Jesus' birth. And in chapter 3, we'll investigate the figure of John the Baptist and delve into the purpose and implications of Jesus' baptism.

1

Jesus' Genealogy

FOCUS TEXT—MATTHEW 1:1–17

*I*t is the year 2033, and you find yourself in an elementary school gymnasium in French Lick, Indiana. A youth league basketball game has just ended, and you are introduced to a ten-year-old standout named Lorenzo Le'Gend. Although he was born and raised in French Lick, Lorenzo explains that he is of Irish descent (his mother's side). He also has a couple of famous ancestors, and his genealogical history reveals some rather intriguing patterns.

You discover that Lorenzo's great-great-great-great-grandfather is Dr. James Naismith, the man who invented the game of basketball in 1891. Naismith's sport caught on quickly, and in the decades following its introduction, semi-professional teams began to emerge in the larger metropolitan areas. Boston's first basketball club, the predecessor to the modern day Celtics team, was established 33 years after the game's creation. The city teams gradually organized into a league—the National Basketball Association—that held regularly scheduled games and year-end playoffs. Thirty-three years following the formation of Boston's club team, the Celtics won their first NBA title. This was the same season that Larry Bird, Lorenzo's great-great-uncle, was born.

Larry made NBA history when the Celtics signed him as a rookie for $3.3 million. By the time he retired as a player, Larry had won the league's MVP Award three consecutive times and had led his franchise to three NBA Championships. Thirty-three years following Larry's departure from the game, Lorenzo was born.

Someone completely unfamiliar with basketball might find Lorenzo's background mildly interesting. It would certainly explain the boy's own fondness for the sport. But a serious hoops fan would suspect something more. They would likely conclude that Lorenzo Le'Gend is destined to become the next Larry Bird. Why? All of the signs point to it. Lorenzo is related not only to the founder of basketball, but also to Bird. His genealogy is permeated with 33s—Bird's number throughout his professional career. Lorenzo is Irish (a true Celt) and was born in French Lick—the inconspicuous birthplace of the sharp-shooting Hall of Famer. Even his name betrays his role. Boston fans dubbed Bird "Larry Legend"—a nickname he certainly lived up to.

Of course, the link between the NBA superstar and the young boy is intentional. In fact, the details above were carefully selected and some of the information was manipulated in order to produce all the 33s. Even so, apprehending the relationship depends largely on one's familiarity with the game. The explanation given enables virtually anyone to make the connection. However, die-hard fans would hardly require that much information. A condensed form of Lorenzo's genealogy would convey the very same message:

> There were 33 years from Dr. Naismith's invention to the founding of Boston's club. There were 33 years from Boston's club to the Celtics' first NBA title. There were 33 years from the Celtics' first title to Larry Bird's retirement. There were 33 years from Bird's retirement to the birth of Lorenzo Le'Gend.

The connection between Larry and Lorenzo is promoted not only by the salient features of this genealogy; for Celtics loyalists, it is also fueled by an underlying desire to return to the glory days of NBA championships. Boston has won more NBA Finals than any other team in history. However, since Bird's exit (and up until the writing of this book) the team has failed to claim even a single conference title. For years, the Celtics faithful have wondered who will be their next Larry Bird. Lorenzo's promising genealogy would certainly invigorate such expectations.

Of course, the plight of an NBA team has nothing to do with Jesus or the NT. Or does it? As it turns out, the gospel of Matthew presents Jesus' genealogy in a way that closely parallels the scenario above. The gospel opens with a very brief introduction:

> The book of the genealogy of Jesus Christ, the son of David, the son of Abraham. (Matt 1:1 NAB)

It then plunges directly into Jesus' historical lineage:

Abraham became the father of Isaac, Isaac the father of Jacob, Jacob the father of Judah and his brothers. Judah became the father of Perez and Zerah. (Matt 1:2–3 NAB)

This ancestral list continues on for fourteen verses, until it reaches Joseph, the husband of Mary. Of her is born Jesus, who is called the Messiah (Matt 1:16). Matthew concludes that

Thus the total number of generations from Abraham to David is fourteen generations; from David to the Babylonian exile, fourteen generations; from the Babylonian exile to the Messiah, fourteen generations. (Matt 1:17 NAB)

The three divisions of fourteen generations are striking. It is possible, of course, that the symmetrical patterns in Jesus' family tree are coincidental. However, the external evidence suggests otherwise. For instance, the genealogy in 1 Chronicles 1–3 identifies precisely the same fourteen generations from Abraham to David, but includes eighteen ancestors between David and the exile. (Matthew has apparently omitted Ahaziah, Jehoash, Amaziah, and Jehoiachim.) Furthermore, Jesus' third set of relatives in Matthew's list (Matt 1:12–16) has been miscounted. Technically, Jesus is the thirteenth generation descending from the exile, not the fourteenth. Even so, this reckoning stands in contrast to the information in Luke—the only other gospel to include Jesus' genealogy. Whereas Matthew has thirteen generations from Shealtiel to Jesus, Luke has twenty-two (Luke 3:23–27).

Matthew evidently took some liberties in order to achieve a triad of fourteen. While this implication may raise concerns of "data tampering," it would hardly have been construed as such back then. In the absence of modernized databases, birth records were difficult to verify. For Matthew, fourteen must have been a decisive number. But what does it stand for? The answer, which escapes present-day readers of the Bible, would have been more obvious to his original Jewish audience. They knew *gematria*.

Gematria refers to an archaic practice that blends literature with math. The Hebrew numerical system employs letters as numbers. It is similar to Roman numerals, where I = 1, V = 5, X = 10, etc. Under this system, the Hebrew letters in any given word also have a numerical value based upon their sum. Ancient authors occasionally wove this value into their writings. For instance, the word *vanity* (*hebel*) has a numerical value of thirty-seven ($h+b+l = 5+2+30 = 37$). In the book of Ecclesiastes, *vanity* appears exactly thirty-seven times. Similarly, Genesis 46 lists the lineage of the sons of Jacob. According to the text, Jacob's seventh son, Gad ($g+d = 3+4 = 7$), bears seven sons. This system can also work in reverse, as is the case in Rev 13:18. The infamous number 666 assigned there to the beast corresponds to the sum of the Hebraic form of Emperor Caesar Nero.

Of course, *gematria* is not always an exact science, especially when one begins with a number. The larger the number is, the greater the pool of possible letter combinations. In the case of Rev 13:18, an additional clue has enabled scholars to pinpoint Nero. The Latinized form of his name yields 616—an alternative reading found in a handful of ancient manuscripts.

Matthew emphasizes the number fourteen. The individual he most likely had in mind was David. Not only does David's name add up to fourteen ($d+v+d = 4+6+4 = 14$), David also appears in the fourteenth position of Jesus' genealogy. Furthermore, of all of Jesus' descendants, only David and Abraham are singled out at both the beginning (Matt 1:1) and the end (1:17) of his list.

The prominence Matthew accords to Abraham is easily explained. Abraham is considered to be the founder of Judaism. The Jews, the progeny of Abraham's second son, Isaac, are heirs to the original covenant made between God and Abraham (Genesis 15, 17). By tracing Jesus' lineage back to Abraham (via Isaac), Matthew is able to both certify and underscore Jesus' Jewishness.

But what accounts for Matthew's interest in David? According to Jewish tradition, David was God's specially appointed king of Israel (1 Sam 16:12–13). But so was Saul (1 Sam 10:1). As king, David demonstrated tremendous zeal in his devotion and service to God (e.g., 2 Sam 6:14–23). But so did both Hezekiah (2 Chr 29:2) and Josiah (2 Kgs 23:25). God promised David that his offspring would always have a place on the throne (2 Sam 7:16). But God made this same promise to Solomon (1 Kgs 9:5). In fact, Solomon's wisdom, wealth, and power exceeded David's (1 Kgs 3:11–13). So why would Matthew want to associate Jesus with David?

The answer has more to do with the events following David's reign than during it. In the centuries after his death, Israel's political strength began to wane. First, the kingdom was fractured by a monarchical dispute. Then, a series of weak and corrupt leaders allowed idolatry and other pagan practices to flourish. Such foreign influences threatened the nation's cultural and religious self-identity. Eventually, the very existence of the Jews was imperiled when rival Near Eastern superpowers—first the Assyrians and then the Babylonians—conquered the region.

The decline of the state was paralleled by a rise in prophetic activity. As the civil conditions deteriorated, the prophets of Yahweh encouraged the Jews with visions of a brighter future. Many of the things the prophets foresaw were renewed elements of Israel's history. According to them, God promised to bring about a new people with new hearts and spirits under a new covenant. God would reestablish a new temple and a new Jerusalem. The Almighty even pledged to raise up a new leader to guide his people. The prophets refer to this individual as the *Messiah*, or "the anointed one." This title is in reference to the ancient practice of anointing a king's head with oil to mark his inauguration.

The expectation of a messiah raises the question of recognition. How would the people know this new leader? What would he look like? The prophetic oracles demonstrate remarkable consistency in their depictions of him. According to the prophets, the Messiah will be none other than the new David:

> See, a time is coming—declares the LORD—when I will raise up a true branch of David's line. He shall reign as king and shall prosper, and he shall do what is just and right in the land. (Jer 23:5 NJPS)

> [I]nstead, they shall serve the LORD their God and David, the king whom I will raise up for them. (Jer 30:9 NJPS)

> Then I will appoint a single shepherd over them to tend them—My servant David. He shall tend them, he shall be a shepherd to them. I the LORD will be their God, and My servant David shall be a ruler among them—I the LORD have spoken. (Ezek 34:23–24 NJPS)

> My servant David shall be king over them; there shall be one shepherd for all of them. They shall follow My rules and faithfully obey My laws. Thus they shall remain in the land which I gave to My servant Jacob and in which your fathers dwelt; they and their children and

their children's children shall dwell there forever, with My servant David as their prince for all time. (Ezek 37:24–25 NJPS)

Afterward, the Israelites will turn back and will seek the LORD their God and David their king—and they will thrill over the LORD and over His bounty in the days to come. (Hos 3:5 NJPS)

As these passages demonstrate, David's persona became so inextricably tied to the notion of the Messiah that his very name became synonymous with it. Given this premise, Matthew's numerical signals become clear. By emphasizing fourteen . . . fourteen . . . fourteen, Matthew stresses to his readers: DAVID! DAVID! DAVID! In other words, Jesus is the new David. Jesus is the long-awaited Messiah.

There are at least two other elements that enable Matthew to solidify the association between David and Jesus. The first has to do with the location of Jesus' birth. Matthew reports that Jesus was born in Bethlehem of Judea (Matt 2:1). According to Mic 5:1, Bethlehem was about as inconspicuous a place as French Lick, Indiana. But it was also David's hometown. Ironically, its backwater status makes it an ideal link between David and Jesus. Never again would this unassuming little village languish in obscurity.

The second element has to do with Jesus' name. From the outset, Matthew refers to him as Jesus "Christ" (1:1). *Christ* comes from the Greek verb *chrio,* meaning "to anoint." It literally means "the anointed one," equivalent to the Hebrew *messiah.* In preparation for his kingship, David was anointed on three separate occasions (1 Sam 16:13; 2 Sam 2:4; 5:3). By referring to Jesus as Christ, Matthew identifies him also as the anointed one. But Jesus' anointing is not in name only. Toward the end of his ministry, following his kinglike procession into Jerusalem (David's capital city), a woman with an alabaster jar anoints Jesus' head with oil (Matt 26:7).

In summary, just as Lorenzo's name, birthplace, and numerical genealogy herald the arrival of the new Larry Bird, Matthew uses these same three components to identify Jesus as the new David. The expectation of Celtics fans in light of the team's prior success and present collapse parallels the anticipation among the Jews in light of their nation's glorious history and first-century struggles. For Matthew, therefore, the messianic promises of old finally met their fulfillment in Jesus. All of the signs point to it.

Before leaving the topic of Matthew's genealogy, there is one more peculiarity here worth mentioning. The Bible contains dozens of ancestry lists (the primary ones occur in Genesis 5; 10; 11; 25; 46; Exodus 6; Numbers 3; 26; Ruth 4; 1 Chronicles 1–9; Ezra 8; Nehemiah 11–12; and Luke 3). Women are rarely named in these records, except when it is necessary to distinguish a patriarch's offspring among multiple wives (as in Genesis 46). In light of this tendency, it becomes noteworthy that Matthew has included among Jesus' forefathers five females: Tamar, Rahab, Ruth, the wife of Uriah (Bathsheba), and Mary. For those unfamiliar with these characters, their inclusion appears altogether random. However, the common traits that tie them together serve to explain Matthew's break from tradition.

Tamar was the daughter-in-law of Judah (the son of Jacob and stepbrother of Joseph). Tamar became a widow when her husband, Er (Judah's eldest son), died. In accordance with Jewish law (Deut 25:5–10), Tamar was given to Er's brother, Onan, so that through him she could bear children in Er's name. However, Onan refused to consummate with Tamar, so the Lord struck him down. Tamar returned to Judah for his third son, Shelah. Judah, afraid that Shelah would meet the same fate as Er and Onan, kept putting Tamar off. Years passed, but Tamar would not be dissuaded. Taking matters into her own hands, she disguised herself as a harlot and enticed Judah to sleep with her. Later, when Judah discovered that Tamar was pregnant, he threatened to have her killed. However, once Tamar produced evidence indicating that the child was his, Judah recanted. He concluded that she was more right than he, since he did not give her to Shelah (Gen 38:1–26).

Rahab was a harlot in Jericho at the time when the Hebrews were poised to enter the promised land. In preparation for their invasion, Joshua sent two spies on a reconnaissance mission into the city. The spies lodged with Rahab, but news of their presence soon reached the king. The king ordered Rahab to put the spies out. At great personal risk, she denied knowledge of their whereabouts while they hid on her roof. Rahab feared the God of the Hebrews, and asked the spies to spare her household when they conquered Jericho. Because of her loyalty, Rahab's request was honored, and she and her kin were adopted into the Israelite community (Josh 2:1–21; 6:20–25).

Ruth and Orpah were Naomi's daughters-in-law. Naomi and her sons were Israelites, but Ruth and Orpah were Moabites. Tragically, Naomi's husband and sons died, and the three widows were left destitute. Naomi encouraged Ruth and Orpah to return to their people in Moab, where the food was more plentiful. However, Ruth refused to leave Naomi, even unto death. The two traveled together to Bethlehem, where Ruth scavenged the ears of grain left behind by the harvesters of Boaz's field. Boaz, a relative of Naomi's, inquired about Ruth and learned of her remarkable fidelity to Naomi. Boaz instructed Ruth to remain in his field and ordered his servants to drop extra grain for her to glean. Following Naomi's instructions, Ruth then pursued Boaz as her husband. One evening, Ruth bathed herself, put on her best attire, and waited until Boaz had had his fill of food and drink. Ruth then stole up next to him and lay down at his feet. When Boaz discovered her in the middle of the night, he enjoined her to remain with him until morning and promised to claim her as his wife the very next day. Ruth stayed, and Boaz kept his pledge. Ruth and Naomi were thus added to his household (Ruth 1–4).

Bathsheba was the wife of Uriah, the armor-bearer of Joab (the commander of David's army). While Joab and Uriah were away on a military campaign, David spied Bathsheba bathing. Captivated by her beauty, he had her brought to his palace where he had relations with her. Shortly thereafter, Bathsheba sent word to David that she was pregnant. David had Uriah called back from the fighting, hoping to get him to sleep with his wife. However, Uriah refused to enjoy her comforts because of the solidarity he felt toward the men in his division. Not to be deterred, David sent Uriah back to the battle, with the order that he be deserted on the front lines. Joab obeyed, Uriah was killed, and Bathsheba moved into the palace. However, God punished David and Bathsheba for their crime, and Bathsheba's child was stillborn. The two repented, God forgave them, and Bathsheba bore David another son, Solomon. Bathsheba eventually intervened on behalf of Solomon. Because of her, it was Solomon—not his brother, Adonijah—who succeeded David as the next king of Israel (2 Samuel 11–12; 1 Kings 1–2).

The histories of these four women converge in a couple of areas. First, each of them engages in sexually questionable behavior. Tamar and Rahab participate in prostitution and Bathsheba in adultery.

Only Ruth could be considered "innocent," although even her actions raise suspicions of impropriety, especially in ancient times.[1] Despite this trend, the Jewish tradition remembers each of these females as heroines.[2] All four of these women were willing to risk their own lives because of their unswerving devotion to the bloodline (Tamar), the God (Rahab), the people (Ruth), and the kingdom (Bathsheba) of Israel.

It is against this background that the fifth woman in Matthew's genealogy—Mary—can be properly understood. Like her predecessors, Mary would also have been seen as sexually questionable. A virgin birth, after all, was far from commonplace! And since adultery was a capital crime (under the law, her betrothal to Joseph would have counted as marriage), her allegiance to God would jeopardize her life. By associating Mary with these particular women, Matthew appears to anticipate her role in Israelite history. Despite (or rather *because of*) her scandalous circumstances, Mary was "in line" to become the next Jewish heroine.

2

Jesus' Nativity Stories

FOCUS TEXTS—MATTHEW 1:18–2:23; LUKE 1:26–2:40

When you think of Christmas, what comes to mind? Santa Claus in his workshop with his busy elves afoot and trusty reindeer on standby? Fresh cut evergreen trees with twinkling lights, dangling ornaments, and neatly wrapped presents heaped underneath? Festive family gatherings? Savory foods and spiced drinks? Newly fallen snow? Caroling? Mistletoe? Innumerable traditions surround this holiday. Chief among them, however, are those timeless Christmas stories that, in their effort to capture the essence of the season, have permanently endeared themselves to the popular imagination. For example, who can forget this holiday tale?

It's a Wonderful Carol

There once lived a man by the name of Ebenezer Bailey. From his youth, Bailey yearned to see the world and to seek his fortune in the most exotic and remote destinations imaginable. However, due to circumstances beyond his control, Bailey was forced to abandon his dreams. Reluctantly, he settled down in his hometown, where he became the manager of the community's savings and loan. With his business, Bailey assisted countless neighbors, but his resentment over his lost opportunities never subsided.

One Christmas Eve, Bailey's bookkeeper, Billy Cratchit, implored Bailey to allow him to take the next day off. Cratchit wanted to spend Christmas with his wife and children (including his crippled son, Tiny Tim). Bailey resisted the idea, but allowed Cratchit to go on the condition that he made the monthly deposit first. Cratchit departed with the envelope of funds, but absentmindedly misplaced it. When the bank examiner arrived at the savings and loan later that afternoon, Bailey became frantic. Without that deposit, Bailey's business would go under and he himself would be subject to criminal indictment.

Bailey returned to his home that night, somewhat hysterical. As he readied himself for bed, Bailey was haunted by the ghost of his former business partner, Jacob Marley. Marley had been doomed to roam the earth wearing heavy chains forged by his own greed. He warned Bailey about suffering a similar fate. Beginning at midnight, Bailey was then visited by three spirits who showed him scenes from Christmases past, present, and future. So gloomy were these visions that he rushed from his house, intending to throw himself off of a bridge.

At the bridge, Bailey witnessed Clarence, an angel out to earn his wings, jump into the frigid waters below. Forgetting about his own suicide, Bailey saved Clarence. Clarence then showed Bailey what his town would have looked like had Bailey never been born. Distressed by what he saw, Bailey begged Clarence for another chance at life. His wish was granted.

Upon returning home, Bailey discovered that his neighbors had all pitched in to cover the missing deposit. He was so overjoyed that he bought the prize turkey in the market and had it sent to the Cratchit's house. Bailey's change of heart allowed Clarence to earn his wings and prompted Tiny Tim to exclaim, "God bless us, every one!"

Most readers will have readily perceived that what appears above is, in fact, not one Christmas story, but two. Elements from Frank Capra's movie *It's a Wonderful Life* (1946) and Charles Dickens' classic *A Christmas Carol* (1843) have been woven together to create a single narrative. These choices were fairly deliberate. The numerous similarities between these two stories lend themselves well to consolidation: Both works relate a dramatic plot that culminates at Christmas. Their main characters are the proprietors of their own businesses. They are both visited by otherworldly beings on Christmas Eve and are troubled by the visions that they are shown. As a consequence, both plead for second shots at life. They are granted their requests and are exceedingly grateful. By the end of the stories, our heroes emerge with a deeper appreciation for the gift of their own lives and a profound new understanding of the "true meaning" of Christmas.

Given all the similarities, one might assume that the unified version would be a completely acceptable substitute for the independent accounts. Yet this is hardly the case. Few would prefer the meganarrative instead of its originals. Why? One reason is that combining the elements of the two separate stories inevitably obscures their distinctive meanings. The lessons rooted in each story cannot emerge until they become disentangled. Consider, once again, *A Christmas Carol* and *It's a Wonderful Life*. Commonalties aside, their fundamental points are almost completely opposite.

In Dickens's account, Ebenezer Scrooge looks back on a life lived selfishly. His failure to reach out to others has prevented him from becoming truly happy. He learns how imperative it is that he change his ways. The aim of Dickens's work, therefore, is to challenge the Scrooges of this world to reconsider their existences and to modify their lifestyles accordingly.

George Bailey's case is altogether different. He *has* lived his life for others. Having seen what would have happened had he never been born, he begins to appreciate his seemingly insignificant contributions to society. He learns how imperative it is that he *not* change (or even *desire* to change) his existence. The goal of this story, therefore, is to assure the George Baileys of the world that despite their personal frustrations and doubts they really do have "a wonderful life."

Perhaps because *A Christmas Carol* and *It's a Wonderful Life* are such popular and contemporary works, we can readily recognize (and rightfully oppose) their amalgamation. Yet when it comes to other Christmas stories—namely, those of Jesus' birth—we commonly intermingle two vastly different versions without realizing it.

To demonstrate this claim, take a moment to recall those elements traditionally associated with the first Christmas—elements that are represented in greeting cards, holiday plays, ornaments, church hymns, television specials, crèche sets, etc. If you were asked to make a list, it may well look something like the one on the next page.

Of the four NT gospels, only two of them—Matthew and Luke—contain stories of Jesus' birth. *Neither* of these accounts contains *all* of the elements listed below. Some of them belong exclusively to Matthew; others are found only in Luke. Very few of them

Elements of the First Christmas		
▪ Mary	▪ a census	▪ shepherds
▪ no room in the inn	▪ the magi	▪ massacre of infants
▪ Joseph	▪ King Herod	▪ dreams
▪ the manger	▪ Bethlehem	▪ Egypt
▪ angels	▪ virgin birth	▪ gold, frankincense,
▪ the star	▪ swaddling clothes	myrrh

are found in both. Therefore, what many take to be *the* story of Jesus' nativity is, in fact, the fusion of two originally independent narratives. Unfortunately, these two narratives have become so thoroughly harmonized that their fundamental (and somewhat opposite) messages about Jesus are all but imperceptible. In order to reclaim these messages, we need to first uncouple one account from the other.

Matthew's Nativity

Matthew's nativity is written primarily from Joseph's perspective. Joseph discovers Mary's pregnancy and decides to divorce her. Joseph is then instructed by God in a dream to take Mary as his wife. This is the first of several dreams Joseph receives. He is also told to name the child "Jesus," to flee for Egypt, to return to Israel, and to settle in Nazareth. Throughout this story, it is Joseph who is given much of the spotlight. This emphasis even translates mathematically: Joseph is explicitly named twice as often as Mary.

Matthew records no details of the birth itself. Instead, he focuses on the dramatic arrival of magi (astrologers) "from the East," traditionally the region of Persia. (The distance that they travel and the time it takes them to do so—up to two years according to Herod's estimation—suggest a group larger than three.) Their claim that the universe itself has disclosed the advent of the new King of the Jews upsets not only Herod, whose reign—and the reign of his descendants—is now threatened, but also "all of Jerusalem." Immediately, Herod convenes assemblies and secret councils. Information is gathered. Calculations are made. Deals are struck.

When the magi leave Jerusalem, the star emblazons their way to Jesus' house. There, they prostrate themselves and do him homage before offering him treasures befitting his royalty (gold), his divinity (frankincense), and his mortality (myrrh). In returning to their native land, the magi evade Herod, who first becomes angry and then grows desperate. In an attempt to secure his throne, he systematically eradicates every child who matches Jesus' profile. Herod's ploy fails, however, because Joseph has already whisked his family away under the cover of darkness to Egypt. Jesus will remain there until Herod's death.

With these details, Matthew leaves his readers with a very specific impression of Jesus' birth. It is portentous. Dramatic. High profile. Political. His advent is signaled throughout the cosmos, and all of Jerusalem is shaken by the news. While foreign dignitaries arrive to pay him tribute, the power structure orders his assassination. This is no ordinary birth. This is the birth of a king.

Matthew's narrative further suggests that this is no ordinary king. Numerous elements from Jesus' birth parallel events and figures from Israel's history. At least four such parallels would have been immediately evident to the typical first-century Jewish reader.

The first parallel concerns Jesus' father. According to Matthew, Joseph receives divine revelations in the form of dreams. Joseph is then responsible for bringing his family to Egypt. In the book of Genesis (chs. 37–46), there is a patriarch who—coincidentally enough—is also named Joseph. He, too, receives divine revelations in the form of dreams and is likewise responsible for bringing his family (the twelve tribes of Israel) to Egypt. That Matthew deliberately sought to associate these two individuals is further evidenced in his genealogy. Whereas Luke 3:23 records the name of Joseph's father (Jesus' paternal grandfather) as "Heli," Matt 1:16 has it as "Jacob." Obviously, a person can only have one biological father. Why the discrepancy? Matthew's version echoes the Genesis story, where "Jacob" is the name of Joseph's father as well!

The second parallel concerns the location of Jesus' birth. The chief priests and scribes were able to determine that the Messiah would be born in Bethlehem because Bethlehem was David's birthplace. As mentioned in chapter 1, since the Messiah was thought to be the "new David," it would be only natural to assume that he would originate from the same city. Jesus' birth in Bethlehem thus strengthens the association between Jesus and David.

The third parallel has to do with the circumstances of Jesus' birth. After Herod learns from the magi that a new king is born, he orders the death of all the males in the vicinity of Bethlehem two years old and under. This event recalls Pharaoh's decree at the time of Moses' birth requiring all newborn Hebrew males to be put to death (Exod 1:15–22). Nonbiblical sources bring these parallels into even closer alignment. According to Josephus (a Jewish historian and contemporary of Matthew), Pharaoh issued this decree precisely in response to a warning by one of his "wise men" that a savior would soon be born to the Israelites (*Ant.* 2.205–207). The circumstances of Jesus' birth, therefore, echo those of Moses'.

The fourth parallel follows the sequence of Jesus' life. In Matthew's gospel, the first significant episode after Jesus leaves Egypt is his baptism (Matt 3:1–17). Once Jesus emerges from the water, he is led into the desert where he remains for forty days and forty nights (Matt 4:1–11). This order of events recalls the Israelites' exodus from Egypt. According to the book of Exodus (chs. 12–14), after the Hebrews come up out of Egypt, their first stop is the Red Sea. God parts this obstacle, so that they, too, emerge from its waters. They are then led into the desert where they sojourn for forty years.

Collectively, these four parallels allow Matthew to underscore Jesus' affinity with the people of Israel. This particular newborn is not merely Jewish; he is personally reliving the experience of the Jews. His coming has caused history to repeat itself, so that the ancient saga of God's chosen people unfolds once again in the profound circumstances of his life. Clearly, this is no ordinary king! This can only be the King of the *Jews,* the Messiah.

Luke's Nativity

Luke provides us with a completely different take on Jesus' birth. To begin with, Luke's story is framed primarily from Mary's perspective. Mary is visited by the angel Gabriel, who announces that she will conceive a child and instructs her to name him "Jesus." Mary questions Gabriel, but eventually consents to God's plan. Mary visits her elderly cousin, Elizabeth, who is also pregnant. Mary remains with Elizabeth for three months, and then returns to her home in Nazareth. From Nazareth, Mary accompanies Joseph to

Bethlehem to be enrolled in the census decreed by Caesar Augustus. While in Bethlehem, she gives birth to Jesus. She wraps him in swaddling clothes and lays him in a manger. When shepherds arrive and explain how angels appeared to them while they were out in the fields, Mary remembers their words and ponders them in her heart. And when the family offers a pair of birds for the purification sacrifice at the temple in Jerusalem, it is to Mary that a prophecy about Jesus is given. Luke's attention to Mary exceeds even Matthew's attention to Joseph. In Luke's nativity, Mary is mentioned *four times* as often as Joseph!

Much of the drama found in Matthew's account is notably absent from Luke's. It is, of course, not altogether insignificant that Jesus' birth is heralded by angels. However, their broadcast is extremely limited, and their recipients are decidedly common. Take Mary, for instance. Twice, Luke refers to her as a female slave, or maidservant (Luke 1:38, 48). In her hymn of praise, she identifies herself with those of "low estate" (1:48 RSV), those of "low degree" (1:52 RSV), and with "the hungry" (1:53 RSV). Indeed, even her offering of the two birds in the temple seems to belie her socioeconomic status. According to the book of Leviticus:

> When the days of [a woman's] purification for a [newborn] son or for a [newborn] daughter are fulfilled, she shall bring to the priest at the entrance of the meeting tent a yearling lamb for a holocaust and a pigeon or a turtledove for a sin offering. The priest shall offer them up before the LORD to make atonement for her, and thus she will be clean again after her flow of blood. Such is the law for the woman who gives birth to a boy or a girl child. If, however, she cannot afford a lamb, she may take two turtledoves or two pigeons, the one for a holocaust and the other for a sin offering. The priest shall make atonement for her, and thus she will again be clean. (Lev 12:6–8 NAB)

Evidently, Mary and Joseph could not even afford the yearling lamb normally required by the law.

Then there are the shepherds, the other recipients of the angelic revelation. Luke's opinion of them remains debatable. According to the Old Testament (OT), both Moses and David were shepherds, and God is frequently portrayed as shepherding his people Israel. On the other hand, shepherds at that time generally had a reputation for being shifty and dishonest (which makes the image of the "Good

Shepherd" all the more poignant). Most likely, Luke's shepherds are to be understood along the lines of Mary: they are commoners. The shepherds are blue-collar locals, hearty and rugged enough to brave both predators and elements in the open country beyond the outskirts of town. Whereas Matthew's gift-bearing ambassadors took up to two years to arrive from their faraway land, the shepherds, we are told, wandered in within a few hours. There was nothing grand about them. Then again, there was nothing grand about the scene they witnessed, either.

Mary and Joseph had been forced to travel. According to Luke, they were not fleeing some half-crazed despot. Rather, they—along with the rest of the world—were merely complying with the Roman census. Finding no vacancy in Bethlehem, Mary was forced to give birth to Jesus outside of a lodge, near a manger. (A manger, of course, is a feeding trough designed to hold fodder for livestock.) Luke does not specify precisely where the manger was located—only that it was outside of the inn. Western tradition envisions the manger in a barn or stable, but the more common practice in the Middle East would have been to situate it in a cave or under a rocky overhang to keep the fodder dry. A manger is a fine receptacle for straw or hay. It is a downright ignoble container in which to put a newborn. Therefore, the very notion that one would find there the Messiah, the Son of God, verges on sacrilege!

Yet this is the type of messiah that Luke endeavors to portray. Relatively little human fanfare accompanies his birth. He enters this world modestly. Unassumingly. Humbly. While "the whole world" goes about its business, the Son of God quietly arrives in the back alley behind some hostel. Not even a crib is spared for this occasion. The infant rests in a paltry feedbox while a few scruffy herdsmen shuffle in to pay their respects.

With his introduction, Luke speaks volumes about who Jesus is and why he has come. Luke's Jesus is not sent as some distinguished monarch to be venerated and revered by a few. Rather, he has come for all—but especially for the poor and the lowly. Because he enters human history as one of them, they too have a privileged claim to his "kingdom" (Luke 5:20).

Given Luke's portrayal of Jesus, one question now remains. To whom does Luke write? Unlike Matthew, Luke probably didn't have a Jewish audience in mind. One clue to Luke's intended au-

II

Jesus' Public Ministry

Having investigated some of the assumptions behind each evangelist's portrayals of Jesus' early years, we have set the stage for the second section of this book: Jesus' public ministry. Four chapters are devoted to this subject. The first (ch. 4) will examine the premises that underlie the more general ministerial frameworks of each of the gospels. The next three (chs. 5–7) will demonstrate how understanding the background improves the understanding of individual episodes from Jesus' public career. Samples of Jesus' parables (ch. 5), teachings (ch. 6), and works (ch. 7) will be considered in turn.

dience can be found in the introduction to this gospel. There, Luke addresses "Theophilus," a Greek name meaning "lover of God (1:3). Although scholars disagree over whether "Theophilus" was a specific individual (perhaps a Roman official) or simply a generic designation for any of Luke's readers, they do agree that the name itself implies a Gentile audience. This assessment is corroborated by certain details in Luke's nativity. For instance, Luke's narrative action transpires not under King Herod, but under the dominion of the Roman authorities—Caesar Augustus and Quirinius (2:1–2). These rulers would have been much more pertinent to a non-Jewish audience.

Assessing the Nativities' Similarities and Differences

Now that we have successfully distinguished Matthew's account from Luke's, we can summarize some of their characteristics with the table on the next page. Our preceding discussion and accompanying table may leave the reader with the impression that these stories have absolutely nothing in common. However, there are some details on which both gospels agree. Both report that a woman named Mary was betrothed to a descendant of David by the name of Joseph. Both explain that before Mary had relations with Joseph, she conceived a son through the Holy Spirit. Both state that Mary gave birth to her son in the town of Bethlehem, and that the child was named Jesus. Both also indicate that Jesus grew up in Nazareth.

Nevertheless, as we have seen, the variations between the two stories far exceed their similarities. Moreover, these variations help to underscore the peculiar message of each gospel. For Matthew, Jesus is the King of the Jews whose dramatic arrival befits his royal status. For Luke, Jesus is the Son of God whose meager circumstances reflect his solidarity with even the most insignificant members of society.

These seemingly opposite portrayals are the result of each writer's premise. Just as Dickens and Capra portrayed the "true meaning of Christmas" differently, depending on whether they were addressing the Ebenezer Scrooges or the George Baileys of this world, so the nativity stories can likewise be understood in light of

Nativity Stories Compared

MATT 1:18–2:23	FEATURES	LUKE 1:26–2:40
Joseph	parental perspective	Mary
dreams	means of divine communication	angels
the Holy Spirit	means of incarnation	the Holy Spirit
magi	visitors	shepherds
star	sign(s) of birth	swaddling clothes, manger
house	place of visit	outside the inn
King Herod	ruler(s)	Caesar Augustus, Quirinius
all of Jerusalem	Who else knows?	very few
Bethlehem	starting point	Nazareth
Egypt	journey	Bethlehem, Jerusalem
Nazareth	return	Nazareth
massacre of the infants	reason for travel	census
ruling class	socioeconomic status	lower class
high-profile, royal, political birth	general impression	low-profile, humble, unassuming birth
Jewish	primary audience	Gentile

each writer's intended audience. Matthew sought to present Jesus to a Jewish audience. Luke sought to make him known to a Gentile one. All of this seems to suggest that who Jesus *really* is depends not only upon whom you ask, but also upon who is asking.

3

John the Baptist and Jesus' Baptism

FOCUS TEXTS: MARK 1:1–11; MATTHEW 3:1–17;
LUKE 3:1–22; JOHN 1:1–34

*U*nlike the gospels of Matthew and Luke, the gospel of Mark contains neither Jesus' genealogy nor his birth story. In fact, Mark's "beginning of the gospel of Jesus Christ" (Mark 1:1 NAB) isn't about Jesus at all. Instead, it's about John the Baptist.

John the Baptist

John (the) Baptist appeared in the desert proclaiming a baptism of repentance for the forgiveness of sins. People of the whole Judean countryside and all the inhabitants of Jerusalem were going out to him and were being baptized by him in the Jordan River as they acknowledged their sins. John was clothed in camel's hair, with a leather belt around his waist. He fed on locusts and wild honey. And this is what he proclaimed: "One mightier than I is coming after me. I am not worthy to stoop and loosen the thongs of his sandals. I have baptized you with water; he will baptize you with the holy Spirit." (Mark 1:4–8 NAB)

One might expect a gospel about Jesus to begin with . . . well, Jesus. Or at least with Jesus' parents. But Mark is not alone in his decision to introduce John the Baptist first. The gospels of Luke and John likewise concentrate on him before shifting their attention to Jesus. Even Matthew, the sole exception to this trend, doesn't put the

Baptist off for long. He situates him in chapter 3, where he appears—as in the other gospels—at the beginning of Jesus' public ministry.

Why does each of the evangelists place such emphasis upon John the Baptist? Popular opinion considers John to be Jesus' "forerunner" or "herald." He is *Star Wars'* Obi-Wan Kenobi to Luke Skywalker, *The Matrix's* Morpheus to Neo, *The Tonight Show's* Ed McMahon to Johnny Carson ("Heeeeeeeere's Jesus!"). He generates interest and builds anticipation. Once he has warmed up the crowd, he presents the headliner—the one everyone really came to see. His work accomplished, he fades from the limelight unnoticed, content to let the hero take center stage.

Although this stereotype of John is partially correct, it overlooks the fact that, for the evangelists, this is not John's only—or even primary—function. In fact, at the point in which the gospels have John first encountering Jesus, the aforementioned tasks have already been accomplished.

As we have seen, the gospel of Matthew previously "heralds" Jesus' coming by his genealogy, Joseph's dreams, the star, and the arrival of the magi. In Luke, it is the angel Gabriel who first spreads the news about Jesus. Later, when the infant is presented in the temple, both Simeon, an aged prophet, and Anna, an elderly prophetess, occupy this role (Luke 2:25–38). Even in the gospel of John, the Baptist initially fails to recognize the Messiah. It is the Holy Spirit who descends upon Jesus so that John is able to identify him (John 1:32–34). Only in Mark's gospel does the Baptist function as the principal "forerunner." There must be another reason for John's importance.

Of course, the gospels remember John as the one who baptizes Jesus. We shall return to this event momentarily. But even it fails to completely account for John's significance in the gospels. Consider, for instance, the relative obscurity surrounding the woman who anointed Jesus. Although her action concretized Jesus' title as Christ and Messiah (lit. the "anointed one"), three of the four gospels fail to even mention her name!

Instead, John's prominence in the gospels is probably related to his widespread popularity during the first century. Even before Jesus arrived on the scene, John had a sizable ministry of his own. The writings of Josephus confirm that the Baptist drew considerable crowds and held great influence over the people. In fact, Josephus's *Jewish Antiquities* devotes more space to John than to Jesus! Not only was Jesus attracted to him, but a number of Jesus' own disciples were also disciples of John (John 1:35–42). It is possible, therefore, that the early Christians who first spread the word about Jesus chose to begin with the Baptist as a common frame of reference.

Obviously, John's notoriety has been significantly eclipsed in the two thousand years since the gospels were written. But what accounted for it? Some see a clue in the location of John's ministry. We are told that John appeared in the "wilderness" to "prepare the way of the Lord" (Mark 1:3 RSV). The "wilderness," of course, is the place where God first liberated the Hebrew slaves from their Egyptian taskmasters, and then covenanted with them as his chosen people. By association, the prophets of the OT anticipated the day when God would restore his people by means of a "new exodus," beginning in the wilderness:

> Therefore, behold, I will allure [Israel], and bring her into the wilderness, and speak tenderly to her. . . . And there she shall answer as in the days of her youth, as at the time when she came out of the land of Egypt. (Hos 2:14–15 RSV)

John's location, therefore, may have appealed to those who believed he would usher in this new exodus. However, John's was not the only "voice crying out in the wilderness." Josephus describes a variety of "impostors and deceivers" who "persuaded the multitude to follow them into the wilderness" under the pretense that "they would exhibit manifest wonders and signs . . . performed by the providence of God" (*Ant.* 20.167–68; similarly, *J.W.* 2.258–60). Like John, these individuals met their ultimate demise at the hands of the political authorities.

John did appear to distinguish himself with his "baptism of repentance for the forgiveness of sins." In fact, the fuller Christian notion of baptism does seem to have originated with John. But ancient records indicate that both the Essenes, a Jewish sect of the first century, and the Qumran community, known to us through the Dead Sea Scrolls, had already associated water immersion with repentance, forgiveness, and initiation into a fellowship of believers. Conceptually, at least, John's baptism was not entirely novel.

It seems that John's renown is to be attributed less to what he did than to who he was—or at least, who people took him to be. John was not merely another visionary in the desert advocating ceremonial purification. Rather, John was thought to be none other than the prophet Elijah.

Elijah resided in Israel during the reigns of Ahab, Ahaziah, and Jehoram (ca. 870–850 BCE). During his astonishing career, Elijah predicted both the beginning and the end of a three-year drought, multiplied a widow's flour and oil, raised her son from the dead, and single-handedly defeated 450 prophets of Ba'al in a lethal contest on Mount Carmel (1 Kings 17–22). Moreover, Elijah appeared to achieve all this while wearing a garment of haircloth with a leather belt about his loins (2 Kgs 1:8)! Elijah's relationship to Christianity, however, has more to do with the events at the end of his life than during it.

According to 2 Kings, when Elijah's time had come, he and his understudy, Elisha, made their way to the Jordan River. With his mantle, Elijah struck the waters, which then parted. Once the two had crossed over,

> Elijah said to Elisha, "Ask for whatever I may do for you, before I am taken from you." Elisha answered, "May I receive a double portion of your spirit." "You have asked something that is not easy," he replied. "Still, if you see me taken up from you, your wish will be granted; otherwise not." As they walked on conversing, a flaming chariot and flaming horses came between them, and Elijah went up to heaven in a whirlwind. When Elisha saw it happen he cried out, "My father! My father! Israel's chariots and drivers!" But when he could no longer see him, Elisha gripped his own garment and tore it in two. (2 Kgs 2:9–12 NAB)

Elijah's dramatic departure gave rise to the tradition that he would eventually return. This tradition is explicitly affirmed in the final verses of Malachi, the last of the prophetic books:

> Lo, I will send you Elijah, the prophet, before the day of the LORD comes, the great and terrible day, to turn the hearts of the fathers to their children, and the hearts of the children to their fathers, lest I come and strike the land with doom. Lo, I will send you Elijah, the prophet, before the day of the LORD comes, the great and terrible day. (Mal 3:23–24 NAB)

Orthodox Jews continue to await the coming of Elijah to usher in the "day of the Lord." In fact, as a sign of their anticipation, they set an extra place for him at the Seder meal each Passover. However, the details in the gospels suggest that Elijah has already returned in the person of John the Baptist. At least four factors support their association. First, Elijah was last seen at the Jordan River; this is where John first appears. Second, Elijah wears a hairy garment with a leather belt; John is dressed the same way. Third, Elijah was expected to "turn the hearts" of the people; John proclaims a baptism of "repentance," a word that literally means "to turn one's heart." Fourth, Elijah was to precede "the day of the Lord"; John speaks of a "mighty one" whose way he is sent to prepare.

The Elijah tradition, then, is the premise that underlies the prominent status accorded to John the Baptist in the gospels. In order to verify Jesus as "the Lord," it was necessary for the evangelists to first establish the return of Elijah. Thus, John is important not merely because he introduces Jesus, but because, as the promised Elijah, he signifies who Jesus is. In this respect, the Baptist functions less like Ed McMahon and more like the Arthurian "sword in the stone."

Those readers familiar with the legend of King Arthur may remember how the blade of a powerful sword had been firmly embedded into a stone by ancient magic. Whoever proved able to draw it from its place was destined to be the next King of England. Over the years, many valiant and noble knights attempted the task, but none were successful. None, that is, until young Arthur, on a mission to replace his brother's misplaced saber, unwittingly freed it. The emergence of the sword revealed Arthur's true identity as the King of England. In much the same way, the reemergence of the prophet Elijah serves to reveal Jesus' true identity as the Lord.

But was John *really* Elijah? Given the gospel writers' knowledge of the OT tradition, it is only natural to wonder to what extent they understood the relationship between the two. The answer to this question varies from gospel to gospel. Mark, as we have seen, presents a number of compelling parallels between the two. Although he never provides a definitive answer to this question, Mark leans toward their mutual identification in chapter 9:

> And [the disciples] asked [Jesus], "Why do the scribes say that first Elijah must come?" And he said to them, "Elijah does come first to

restore all things. . . . But I tell you that Elijah has come, and they did to him whatever they pleased, as it is written of him." (Mark 9:11–13 RSV)

Matthew appears less comfortable with such ambiguity. Not once, but twice does Matthew's gospel explicitly confirm that John is Elijah. This makes sense, in light of his predominately Jewish audience.

> For all the prophets and the law prophesied until John; and if you are willing to accept it, he is Elijah who is to come. He who has ears to hear, let him hear. (Matt 11:13–15 RSV)

> And the disciples asked him, "Then why do the scribes say that first Elijah must come?" He replied, "Elijah does come, and he is to restore all things; but I tell you that Elijah has already come, and they did not know him, but did to him whatever they pleased. . . ." Then the disciples understood that he was speaking to them of John the Baptist. (Matt 17:10–13 RSV)

Of course, the tradition of Elijah would not have been nearly as important for Luke's predominately Gentile audience. Therefore, Luke is content to keep their association symbolic. His is the only gospel that records the story of John's birth, thus eliminating the possibility that Elijah simply descended from the heavens. He also omits details such as the hairy garment, the leather belt, and Jesus' insistence that Elijah had returned. Nevertheless, Luke affirms the Baptist's fundamental role as the one who goes before Jesus "in the spirit and power of Elijah" (Luke 1:17 RSV).

The Baptist's function in the gospel of John is similar to the others, in that he appears at the beginning of Jesus' ministry and testifies to Jesus' true identity. However, when the Jews send priests and Levites to inquire whether or not he is Elijah, John answers unequivocally: "I am not" (John 1:21 RSV). Like Luke, then, the author of the Fourth gospel concedes the Baptist's Elijah-like purpose, but resists the notion that John is *actually* Elijah.

Despite the fact that the evangelists vary in their understanding of the precise relationship between John and Elijah, they each accord the Baptist due prominence as the one who authenticates Jesus as the Lord. Just as Arthur's claim to the throne of England would have been futile without the legendary sword, so too would Jesus' anointed status be suspect without the prophetic John.

Having thus established the premise behind John's significance, one task now remains. No treatment of John the Baptist would be complete without addressing the subject of Jesus' baptism and the story behind that story.

Jesus' Baptism

In those days Jesus came from Nazareth of Galilee and was baptized by John in the Jordan. And when he came up out of the water, immediately he saw the heavens opened and the Spirit descending upon him like a dove; and a voice came from heaven, "Thou art my beloved Son; with thee I am well pleased." (Mark 1:9–11 RSV)

A careful reading of Mark's narrative reveals the theological difficulty posed by this event. If John offered a "baptism of repentance for the forgiveness of sins" (Mark 1:4 RSV//Luke 3:3), and Jesus himself submitted to it, doesn't Jesus' action indicate that he had sinned? Some, of course, would answer affirmatively. However, this notion contradicts the early and widespread belief that asserted otherwise:

For our sake he made him to be sin who knew no sin, so that in him we might become the righteousness of God. (2 Cor 5:21 RSV)

Since then we have a great high priest, . . . Jesus, the Son of God, let us hold fast [to] our confession. For we have not a high priest who is unable to sympathize with our weaknesses, but one who in every respect has been tempted as we are, yet [is] without sin. (Heb 4:14–15 RSV)

That the evangelists also suppose Jesus to be blameless is evidenced by the fact that, although they describe everyone else as "confessing their sins" (Mark 1:5 RSV//Matt 3:6), this aspect is completely missing from Jesus' baptism.

In fact, the gospel writers seem acutely aware that Jesus' baptism could cause their readers to draw the wrong conclusion about him. Undoubtedly, this is what prompted some of their alterations. In Matthew's version, for instance, when Jesus comes forward,

John tried to prevent him, saying, "I need to be baptized by you, and yet you are coming to me?" Jesus said to him in reply, "Allow it now, for thus it is fitting for us to fulfill all righteousness." Then he allowed him. (Matt 3:14–15 NAB)

The gospel of John goes even further. According to it, Jesus is not baptized at all! Instead, Jesus is the one who *does* the baptizing (so John 3:22 and 4:1; although cf. 4:2, which appears to be a later emendation).

These concerted efforts to protect Jesus' reputation beg the question, why *was* Jesus baptized? Or, more precisely, if the evangelists believed Jesus to be without sin, how did *they* understand his baptism?

The most common explanation is that Jesus was baptized in order to set an example for others. Unfortunately, this argument proves to be rather whimsical. The gospels are filled with guidelines that Jesus expects his disciples to follow, but Jesus doesn't act out each and every one of them. Why *demonstrate* baptism, especially in light of the mixed message it might send? Furthermore, this solution sheds little light on the divine response that immediately follows. Why does this particular example elicit God's favor above all the others?

Most likely, the evangelists conceived of Jesus' baptism in a completely different way. Their interpretation is based on an understanding that is not immediately obvious to the modern reader. To discern this premise, it helps to try to envision the baptismal scene.

Mark tells us that "*all* the country of Judea, and *all* the people of Jerusalem" were going out to John (Mark 1:5 RSV, emphasis added). Matthew expands this to include "Jerusalem and *all* Judea and *all* the region about the Jordan" (Matt 3:5 RSV, emphasis added). This is a sizable population! Most likely, these people gathered along Jordan's bank. When it was their turn, they waded out to John, publicly confessed their sins, and then were immersed in the river. Once they were baptized, they were, theoretically, free of their sins. But where did their sins "go"? The answer, of course, is *into the water.* (It is not clear whether the evangelists understood this literally or figuratively, but for our purposes here it makes very little difference.)

Now Jesus enters the picture. Again, he is presumably the only one *without* sin. Think of the Jordan as a washbasin. If those who are dirty are rendered clean by its waters, then the one who is clean can only be rendered dirty. In other words, those who are sinful have gone to the Jordan to cast off their sins. However, Jesus, the one who is sinless, goes there to take them up. Jesus' assumption of humanity's offenses will thus enable him to fulfill his mission—a mission devoted to the conquest of sin.

But what of John's gospel? One might recall that in an attempt to spare his audience the "scandal" of Jesus' baptism, John has chosen to omit it. Nevertheless, the *function* of this act has been scrupulously preserved. It appears transformed into an assertion on the lips of John the Baptist as he watches Jesus approach the Jordan River: "Behold, the Lamb of God, who takes away the sin of the world" (John 1:29 RSV).

Given the function of Jesus' baptism, the scene immediately following it in Matthew, Mark, and Luke (collectively known as the Synoptic Gospels because of their similar perspective) begins to make sense. God declares, "This is my beloved Son, with whom I am well pleased!" (Matt 3:16–17 NAB//Mark 1:10–11//Luke 3:21–22). God is not delighted because Jesus, like everyone else, has repented of his wrongdoings. Nor is it because Jesus has provided a particularly helpful demonstration for his followers. Rather, God is especially gratified because Jesus has willingly shouldered the transgressions of all the people. This is the first crucial step toward accomplishing the divine plan.

It is little wonder, then, that the evangelists consider Jesus' baptism such a pivotal event. From this point forward, Jesus will demonstrate his capacity to forgive individuals of their sins, a capacity he does not (and perhaps cannot) exhibit prior to his baptism. Unfortunately, the destruction of these sins will now, by necessity, involve the destruction of Jesus. Assuming that he is not dissuaded—an endeavor Satan immediately undertakes (Mark 1:12–13//Matt 4:1–11//Luke 4:1–13)—Jesus' days will be numbered.

4

Ministerial Frameworks

FOCUS TEXTS: MARK 1:21–8:24; MATTHEW 1–28;
LUKE 1–13; JOHN 2–12

So far, our consideration of premises has focused primarily on the contents of the gospels. But certain presuppositions underlie their *structures* as well. Evidently, each evangelist had at their disposal a wealth of traditions about Jesus, including his teachings, his actions, his healings, etc. While much of this material is common to two, three, or even all four of the gospels, its distinctive arrangement varies from author to author.

A couple of examples can illustrate this point. In the gospels of Matthew, Mark, and Luke, Jesus drives the merchants out of the temple near the conclusion of his ministry (Matt 21:12–13//Mark 11:15–17//Luke 19:45–46). This act incites the Jewish leaders to destroy him (Mark 11:18//Luke 19:47). In the gospel of John, however, this same event occurs near the beginning of Jesus' ministry (John 2:13–17). There, it helps to initiate it. Similarly, in Matthew, Mark, and John, a woman with an alabaster jar anoints Jesus with oil in preparation for his approaching death (Matt 26:6–13//Mark 14:3–9//John 12:1–8). In Luke, however, the anointing takes place in the middle of Jesus' ministry, where it serves as an object lesson in forgiveness (Luke 7:36–50).

The evangelists' arrangements of their gospels are not limited simply to the repositioning of a few individual episodes from Jesus' life. Rather, each of the gospels exhibits its own distinctive framework that underlies Jesus' *entire ministry.* Of course, the notion that the evangelists could take such liberties with the sequence of supposedly historical events may be difficult for modern readers to accept.

But the following analogy may help to clarify the dynamics behind these literary structures.

Think of four realtors who are attempting to sell the same house. Although they all have the same piece of real estate to work with, each one will undoubtedly know more about certain aspects than the others. How they choose to present the property will vary according to their individual preferences and, of course, those of their potential buyers. For instance, one realtor may relish the home's location. Another may be charmed by its historical characteristics. A third may appreciate its progressive adaptations. A fourth may simply admire the architect. How each realtor conducts his or her "walk-through" will be determined, in part, by these inclinations. Where do they begin and in what sequence do they proceed? Which rooms will they breeze by? In which will they linger? Which features will they accentuate? And which will they ignore?

We can liken the individual components of the house to the individual episodes in the gospels. Like the realtors, the evangelists do not simply present these events randomly. Rather, to the extent that they are able, they arrange their materials according to what they think constitutes the most salient qualities of Jesus' ministry. Just as the "structure" of a realtor's walk-through will be predicated upon his perception of the house, so the structure of these gospels are predicated upon their authors' perceptions of Jesus. In this respect, the broader framework of each gospel affords us a unique glimpse into the mind of its writer, and suggests to us what they valued most about the nature of Jesus' public career.

Mark

To most modern readers, Mark's account of Jesus' ministry does not appear to be very well organized. Jesus seems to travel around at random, teaching, healing, and performing other miracles as he goes. However, to a first-century audience familiar with the region, Jesus' travel itinerary would have conveyed much more.

Mark indicates the key to the structure of Jesus' ministry from the very beginning. Jesus starts at the Sea of Galilee (Mark 1:16). Even a casual glance at this gospel confirms the importance of this body of water. Jesus visits the towns in its vicinity, ministers along its shores, and even preaches and performs miracles while sailing upon it. In fact, the word *boat* appears far more often in Mark's gospel (seventeen times) than in any of the other gospels (Matthew, thirteen times; Luke, five times; John, eight times). This statistic is especially impressive, considering that Mark's is the shortest of all.

Although Mark's Jesus gets into boats on a number of occasions (e.g., 3:9; 4:1; 6:32; 8:10), Mark clearly differentiates four major crossings of the Sea of Galilee. These are the only times Mark uses the key phrase "to the other side." In the opening of the gospel, Jesus is on the Galilean, or western, side of the sea (so 1:14). Jesus' first voyage to the eastern side is recorded in 4:35–41. Jesus returns to the western side in 5:21, crosses east again in 6:45–53, and then returns to the western shore for good in 8:13.

When one compares what transpires in conjunction with these four voyages, some intriguing parallels appear. Jesus' first action in western territory, following the calling of his disciples, is to cast unclean spirits out of a man (1:21–27). As a result of this exorcism, Jesus' fame spreads throughout Galilee (1:28). When he first arrives on the eastern side, Jesus again casts out unclean spirits from a man (5:1–19). As a result of this exorcism, his notoriety circulates throughout the Decapolis (a confederation of ten Greco-Roman cities situated on the eastern side of the Sea of Galilee; 5:20).

When Jesus returns to the western shore in 5:21, a large crowd gathers around him, and he is immediately presented with requests for healing. Jesus restores a number of individuals, and then he feeds a crowd of thousands with only a few loaves of bread and a couple of fish (6:34–44). Mark records that the number of baskets of food left over from this event was twelve.

Jesus then returns back to the eastern region. As in his first return to the western side, people likewise gather their sick and solicit his assistance. Again, Jesus cures a variety of maladies, and then feeds another group numbering in the thousands with only a little bread and a few fish (8:1–9). In this case, the sum of the baskets left over is seven.

Why has Mark chosen to organize Jesus' ministry in this manner? And what do all of these parallels mean? Mark alludes to the purpose of this structure in the context of the final crossing (8:13–21). We are told that the disciples "had forgotten to bring bread, and they had only one loaf with them in the boat" (8:14 NAB).

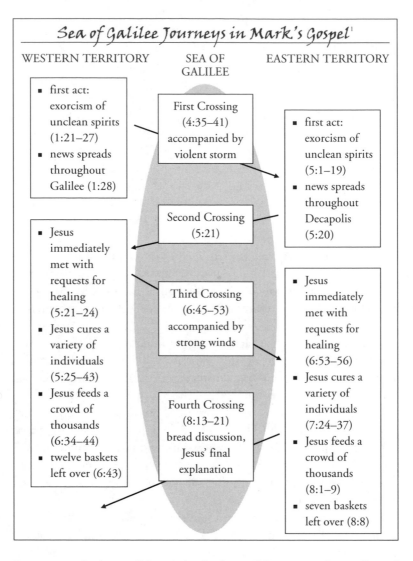

Sea of Galilee Journeys in Mark's Gospel[1]

WESTERN TERRITORY	SEA OF GALILEE	EASTERN TERRITORY
• first act: exorcism of unclean spirits (1:21–27) • news spreads throughout Galilee (1:28)	First Crossing (4:35–41) accompanied by violent storm	• first act: exorcism of unclean spirits (5:1–19) • news spreads throughout Decapolis (5:20)
• Jesus immediately met with requests for healing (5:21–24) • Jesus cures a variety of individuals (5:25–43) • Jesus feeds a crowd of thousands (6:34–44) • twelve baskets left over (6:43)	Second Crossing (5:21) Third Crossing (6:45–53) accompanied by strong winds Fourth Crossing (8:13–21) bread discussion, Jesus' final explanation	• Jesus immediately met with requests for healing (6:53–56) • Jesus cures a variety of individuals (7:24–37) • Jesus feeds a crowd of thousands (8:1–9) • seven baskets left over (8:8)

Jesus reminds them of the twelve baskets of fragments they collected first, and of the seven baskets they collected second (8:19–20). Then he provocatively asks, "Do you still not understand?" (8:21 NAB).

Mark implies that Jesus' disciples did not catch on to what he was doing. However, Mark's original audience almost certainly would have. They would have recognized that the western, Galilean side of the sea was Jewish territory. They also would have associated the eastern side with the Decapolis and the region of the Gentiles.

Thus, they would have concluded that Jesus' parallel actions on either side of the sea demonstrate his desire to reach out to both the Jews *and* the Gentiles. In other words, Jesus wishes to minister equally to both groups. In this respect, Mark portrays Jesus as the "one bread" who has been sent to satisfy the Jews, whose leftover baskets are twelve—a figure often used to designate this group, as in the twelve tribes of Israel. But Jesus' mission finds fulfillment only when it is also extended to the Gentiles, whose leftover baskets are seven—a number often used to connote fulfillment or completion, as in the seven days of the week.

That Jesus' earliest followers experienced difficulty in reaching out to the Gentiles is signified by the two storms that they encounter in their crossings. Each time the disciples endeavor to traverse the Sea of Galilee from its western (Jewish) to its eastern (Gentile) side, the forces of nature oppose their progress (so 4:35–41 and 6:45–53). In both cases, however, Jesus proves himself to be mightier than such opposition. With his assistance, their vessel successfully makes it to the distant shore.

The structure of this gospel thus indicates that Mark understood Jesus' separate but equal outreach to Jews and Gentiles to be the most pivotal feature of his ministry. To return to our analogy, perhaps we can liken Mark to a realtor who is especially attuned to the value of location. He points out that the property is adjacent to both the Chinatown and Little Italy neighborhoods. As such, it lies in close proximity to their respective stores, restaurants, cultural centers, and houses of worship. Thus, he concludes that this home could serve members of either ethnic group equally well. Of course, as we shall see, this is hardly the only way to appreciate this prime piece of real estate. The other evangelists perceive the framework of Jesus' ministry differently.

Matthew

Of all the gospels, Matthew's construction is the most clearly recognizable. Matthew has neatly grouped Jesus' teachings together into a series of five extended discourses, each of which ends similarly. Matthew fills narrative material in between these discourses, so that the general outline looks like this:

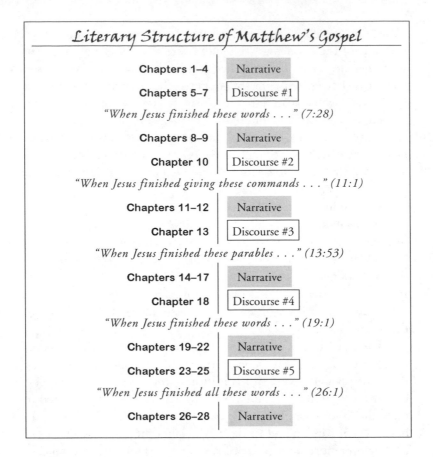

Literary Structure of Matthew's Gospel

Chapters 1–4	Narrative
Chapters 5–7	Discourse #1

"When Jesus finished these words . . ." (7:28)

Chapters 8–9	Narrative
Chapter 10	Discourse #2

"When Jesus finished giving these commands . . ." (11:1)

Chapters 11–12	Narrative
Chapter 13	Discourse #3

"When Jesus finished these parables . . ." (13:53)

Chapters 14–17	Narrative
Chapter 18	Discourse #4

"When Jesus finished these words . . ." (19:1)

Chapters 19–22	Narrative
Chapters 23–25	Discourse #5

"When Jesus finished all these words . . ." (26:1)

Chapters 26–28	Narrative

As this outline suggests, Matthew places a significant emphasis upon Jesus' words. In fact, compared to the gospel of Mark, Matthew's Jesus spends less time healing (Mark, seventeen episodes; Matthew, thirteen episodes), and more time teaching (Mark, three parables; Matthew, twelve parables).

What, then, accounts for Matthew's unique arrangement of his material and his demonstrated interest in Jesus' teachings? The structure itself offers a clue. For a first-century Jewish reader, Jesus' five sermons would most likely call to mind the five books of the Torah (Genesis, Exodus, Leviticus, Numbers, and Deuteronomy)—the heart of the Hebrew Scriptures. It was Moses, of course, who first received the law from God on Mount Sinai (Exodus 19–20). Tradition thus ascribes authorship of this collection to him.

Matthew's divisions suggest that, if Moses was the former law-giver, then Jesus is the new lawgiver. Indeed, this paradigm is steadily reinforced throughout Matthew's gospel. There are, for instance, the parallel circumstances surrounding the births of Jesus and Moses (as previously described in chapter 2). Matthew's Jesus delivers his first set of "commandments"—like Moses—from a mountain (Matt 5:1, but cf. Luke 6:20–49, where this same sermon occurs on a plain). In this gospel, a mountain is also the scene of Jesus' final appearance (Matt 28:16–20), as it was for Moses' (Deuteronomy 34).

Perhaps the clearest affirmation of Jesus' role as the new law-giver, however, is to be found in the content of his first discourse. Here, Jesus embraces the law to a degree that is unparalleled in the other gospels:

> Do not think that I have come to abolish the law or the prophets. I have come not to abolish but to fulfill. Amen, I say to you, until heaven and earth pass away, not the smallest letter or the smallest part of a letter will pass from the law, until all things have taken place. Therefore, whoever breaks one of the least of these commandments and teaches others to do so will be called least in the kingdom of heaven. But whoever obeys and teaches these commandments will be called greatest in the kingdom of heaven. (Matt 5:17–19 NAB; see also 23:1–3)

Jesus proceeds to teach his disciples according to a series of com-parisons between what Moses' law stated—"you have heard it said"—and what Jesus now expects—"but I say to you" (Matt 5:21–48). In each case, Jesus' requirements become more stringent, since he takes intentions, and not just actions, into account.

But why did Matthew go to such trouble to accentuate the rela-tionship between Jesus and Moses? After all, wasn't the Messiah to be patterned after David? The premise of this association would have been clear to Matthew's original audience. As it turns out, the Torah had foretold the coming of another "prophet" like Moses. In Deuter-onomy, Moses tells the people:

> A prophet like me will the LORD, your God, raise up for you from among your own kinsmen; to him you shall listen. . . . And the LORD said to me, "This was well said. I will raise up for them a prophet like you from among their kinsmen, and will put my words into his mouth; he shall tell them all that I command him. If any man will not

listen to my words which he speaks in my name, I myself will make him answer for it." (Deut 18:15–19 NAB)

One might be tempted to understand this promise as referring to Joshua, Moses' successor. But the conclusion of the Torah resists this interpretation. Rather, it assigns to Moses a rather incomparable place in history:

> Since then no prophet has arisen in Israel like Moses, whom the LORD knew face to face. He had no equal in all the signs and wonders the LORD sent him to perform in the land of Egypt . . . and for the might and the terrifying power that Moses exhibited in the sight of all Israel. (Deut 34:10–12 NAB)

Ever since his death, the Jews have been on the lookout for the "prophet like Moses." The structure of this gospel indicates that Matthew took Jesus to be the fulfillment of this expectation. Perhaps for this reason, Matthew's Jesus devotes his public ministry almost exclusively to the Jews (so Matt 10:5–7; 15:22–26). It is only after his rejection, death, and resurrection that he sends his disciples to the Gentiles (so Matt 28:16–20).

Given Matthew's penchant for tradition, we could liken him to a realtor who most appreciates the house's history. Accordingly, he is able to highlight the original features of the building, such as the foundation, the brass fixtures, the oak trim, and the central fireplace. Furthermore, he can explain how these features have been incorporated into a major renovation and are now utilized in the present dwelling. For this realtor, those original features largely define the character of the home. It's left to the two remaining realtors to highlight the construction's progressive adaptations and the architect's signature style.

Luke

With regard to its structure, the gospel of Luke presents a more complex challenge than either Mark or Matthew. To some extent, this is because it constitutes the first volume of a two-part work (the second half being the Acts of the Apostles). Therefore, any comprehensive literary analysis must take both of these texts into consideration. Furthermore, although commentators typically delineate

Luke's version of Jesus' ministry according to Jesus' provincial move-
ments (e.g., the "Galilee Ministry" in Luke 4:14–9:50, and the
"Journey to Jerusalem" in 9:51–19:27), the episodes contained
within do not appear to be as geographically correlated as they are,
for instance, in Mark's gospel.

Instead, Luke tends to weave a number of themes throughout
Jesus' ministry. Among other things, he emphasizes historicity,
prayer, the Holy Spirit, the poor, Samaritans, humility, and compassion. Luke also groups similar material together around common
topics. In 11:1–13, for instance, Luke joins together three different
teachings of Jesus' on prayer (two of which appear independently in
the gospel of Matthew). In 15:1–32, he successively records three
parables about recovering that which is lost.

If Luke's structure can be understood thematically, then there
is one theme that has perhaps the clearest impact upon it. This
theme is expressed through the unique symmetry of Luke's gospel.
In chapter 1, Luke recounts the story of Zechariah's experience in
the temple (Luke 1:5–25). The angel Gabriel appears to Zechariah, who is initially "troubled" by the encounter. Gabriel enjoins
him to "be not afraid" and reveals to him that his wife, who is
barren, will bear a son. Gabriel describes the unique mission for
which this child is destined, and then tells Zechariah what name
to give him: John. In response to this news, Zechariah questions
Gabriel and is consequently struck mute. Eventually, however,
Zechariah regains his speech and offers a canticle of praise to
God (1:67–79).

Next, Luke describes Mary's experience (1:26–56). She, too, is
visited by the angel Gabriel and is "troubled" by his appearance. Gabriel encourages her to "be not afraid" and informs her of her own
miraculous conception, since she is still a virgin. Gabriel explains the
unique mission of her son and tells her what to name him: Jesus.
Mary likewise responds with a question and is consequently given an
answer. Then she delivers her own song of praise.

The parallels between Zechariah and Mary are inescapable.
(One is left only to wonder why Zechariah's question resulted in
punishment while Mary's did not!) This pair, however, is only the
first of many that Luke will introduce throughout his gospel.
Sometimes they appear consecutively, like Zechariah and Mary.
This is how Luke introduces Simeon, the aged prophet (2:25–35),

and Anna (2:36–38), the aged prophetess, who meet the newborn Jesus in the temple. (Another example is Ananias and Sapphira in Acts 5:1–11.) But more often, there is some narrative distance between such pairs. This is especially true in the context of Jesus' ministry.

Mark and Matthew, for instance, include descriptions of the twelve disciples, of Jesus raising the official's daughter from the dead, and of Jesus straightening out a man's hand on the Sabbath. Luke not only mentions these (6:12–16; 8:49–56; 6:6–11), he also supplements each one with a corresponding gender match. Thus, Luke's Jesus has "many other" women followers who provide for him out of their means (8:2–3). He raises a widow's son from the dead (7:11–17), and he straightens a woman's back on the Sabbath (13:10–17). Luke's Jesus even incorporates such pairings into his teachings. He uses both a male hosteller (11:5–8) and an exploited widow (18:1–8) to exemplify persistence in prayer. Likewise, he uses a shepherd who discovers his lost sheep (15:3–7) and a woman who discovers her lost coin (15:8–10) to epitomize heaven's response to the repentance of a lost soul. Luke's symmetry, therefore, can be summarized as in the figure on the next page.

What is the purpose of this narrative structure? Such a diligent balance across gender lines suggests that Luke perceived women as equal participants both in the formation and in the expression of Jesus' ministry. Given the cultural norms of Luke's time, this assertion is fairly bold. Women in the first century were treated as second-class citizens and thus denied many of the rights, freedoms, and opportunities available to men. That Luke accords them such an equivalent role indicates that, at least for this evangelist, Jesus' ministry was able to transcend such biases.

In keeping with our analogy, we could thus compare Luke to the realtor who appreciates the house's progressive adaptations. As he shows the property to a newlywed couple, for instance, he is careful to point out how features such as the two-car garage, the doublewide bathtub, the matching walk-in bedroom closets, and the dual bathroom sinks were all designed to accommodate not only the husband, but also the wife. Although such features would be rare among dwellings from the same era, this home somehow managed to buck the trend.

Gender Symmetry in Luke's Gospel

MALE	FEMALE
Luke 1:5–20	Luke 1:26–38
Zechariah	Mary
Gabriel appears.	Gabriel appears.
He is troubled.	She is troubled.
"Do not be afraid."	"Do not be afraid."
He is told of an unusual birth.	She is told of an unusual birth.
The son will be special.	The son will be special.
He is told to name him John.	She is told to name him Jesus.
He questions Gabriel.	She questions Gabriel.
He sings a song of praise.	She sings a song of praise.
Luke 2:25–35	Luke 2:36–38
Simeon	Anna
prophet	prophetess
meets Jesus in temple	meets Jesus in temple
Luke 7:11–17	Luke 8:49–56
Jesus raises widow's son.	Jesus raises Jairus' daughter.
Luke 6:12–16	Luke 8:1–3
twelve disciples	women followers
Luke 6:6–11	Luke 13:10–17
Jesus straightens a man's hand on the Sabbath.	Jesus straightens a woman's back on the Sabbath.
Luke 11:5–8	Luke 18:1–8
Persistent hosteller is an example of prayer.	Persistent widow is an example of prayer.
Luke 15:3–7	Luke 15:8–10
Shepherd and lost sheep model heaven and lost soul.	Widow and lost coin model heaven and lost soul.

John

Although scholars have found a variety of ways to subdivide John's gospel, most of them acknowledge the structural significance of the seven miracles that Jesus performs. Jesus initiates his ministry by changing water into wine at a wedding in Cana (John 2:1–11). He then cures an official's son (4:46–54), heals a paralytic (5:1–9), multiplies loaves (6:1–15), walks on water (6:16–21), and restores sight to a man born blind (9:1–7). Jesus finally concludes his public work on a truly impressive note—he raises his friend Lazarus from the dead (11:1–44).

Of course, the other gospels include accounts of Jesus' miracles, many of which are either similar or identical to those found here. Yet only John employs such miracles as the organizing principle for Jesus' career. Why?

One clue can be found in the term John uses to describe these acts. Whereas the Synoptic Gospels refer to them as "miracles," John designates them as "signs." In the Torah (and in later Jewish literature), this same term is reserved almost exclusively for the supernatural deeds God performed in Egypt on behalf of his chosen people (see, e.g., Exod 4:28–30; 7:3; 10:1–2; 14:11, 22; Deut 4:34; 6:22; 7:19). In fact, several of Jesus' feats mirror those associated with the exodus: God changed water into blood (Exod 7:4–24); Jesus changes water into wine. God led the Hebrews through the sea (Exod 14:15–32); Jesus leads his disciples through the sea. God fed the people with "bread from heaven" (Exod 16:4–35); Jesus offers his followers "bread from heaven." Jesus' signs, therefore, are founded upon God's actions:

> Amen, amen, I say to you, a son cannot do anything on his own, but only what he sees his father doing; for what he does, his son will do also. For the Father loves his Son and shows him everything that he himself does, and he will show him greater works than these, so that you may be amazed. (John 5:19–20 NAB)

In this respect, John is portraying Jesus as the Messiah, but not as a "new David" or a "prophet like Moses." Rather, John likens Jesus to Yahweh. Jesus is even given this name (17:11–12). On several occasions, Jesus uses the titular "I AM" as a self-designation (4:26; 6:20; 8:24, 28, 58; 13:19; 18:5, 6, 8). This is identical to the divine name first entrusted to Moses on Mount Sinai (Exod 3:14) and employed by later writers in reference to Yahweh (e.g., Isa 41:4; 43:10, 25; 45:18–19; 46:4; 51:12).

In fact, the correspondence between Jesus and Yahweh permeates John's entire gospel. Jesus is the preexistent "Word," who brings all of creation into being (John 1:1–4). He is seen by Abraham (8:56), written about by Moses (5:46), and spoken of by Isaiah (12:41). Jesus' words are God's words (12:49), and Jesus' actions are God's actions (14:10). So close is their relationship that whoever knows Jesus knows God (14:7), whoever has seen Jesus has seen God (14:9), whoever hears Jesus hears God (14:24), whoever loves Jesus is loved by God (14:21), and whoever hates Jesus hates God (15:23). For all practical purposes, Jesus and God are one (10:30; 17:21–22).

That such an extravagant claim would have been considered blasphemous by many Jews of Jesus' time is evidenced by their repeated efforts to stone him (5:18; 8:59; 10:31). However, because the magnitude of Jesus' assertion is matched by the magnitude of his signs, his ministry causes a considerable division among the people (7:12, 40–44; 10:19–21; 12:37–43). They must judge for themselves whether Jesus is who he purports to be.

In this respect, John has written this gospel as if Jesus' claim to be the Son of God is on trial. Indeed, much of John's vocabulary—witness, truth, falsehood, judge, testify, signs, advocate, judgment, condemnation, innocence—lends itself well to this motif. Jesus' signs thus constitute the "evidence" of his intimate relationship with God:

> If I do not perform my Father's works, do not believe me; but if I perform them, even if you do not believe me, believe the works, so that you may realize (and understand) that the Father is in me and I am in the Father. (10:37–38 NAB; see also 14:11)

This is also why Jesus' final sign—his seventh (the raising of Lazarus from the dead)—completes his ministry:

> For just as the Father raises the dead and gives life, so also does the Son give life to whomever he wishes. (5:21 NAB)

Ironically, Jesus' last and most compelling miracle, the one that should have led to his vindication, instead becomes the grounds for his death sentence (11:45–53).

The structure of John's gospel, therefore, serves a narrative purpose. Jesus' signs corroborate his claim to be the Son of God. Some chose to accept this evidence. Others chose to reject it. But the signs also serve a rhetorical purpose, which John explains at the conclusion to his gospel:

> Now Jesus did many other signs in the presence of (his) disciples that are not written in this book. But these are written that you may (come to) believe that Jesus is the Messiah, the Son of God, and that through this belief you may have life in his name. (20:30–31 NAB)

In this way, John ultimately leaves the "verdict" concerning Jesus' claim to be the Son of God up to his readers. The decision now lies with them.

John could be equated with the realtor who is particularly enamored with the house's architect. The features that he appreciates the most—high vaulted ceilings, abundant natural lighting, a reflecting pool, and a prominent wine cellar—most clearly epitomize the master's style. As far as this realtor is concerned, their classical representation in this particular home leaves little doubt as to *whose* work it is. Likewise, given the signs recorded in this gospel, John leaves little doubt as to whose "blueprint" Jesus is following.

Conclusion

As we have seen, the evangelists communicate their understanding of Jesus not only through the content, but also through the structure of their gospels. Each perceives the purpose of Jesus' ministry differently. For Mark, Jesus desires to reach out not only to the Jews, but also to the Gentiles. For Matthew, Jesus is the "prophet like Moses" whose teachings promote and succeed those of the Torah. For Luke, the complementary roles played by women indicate the ability of Jesus' ministry to overcome discriminatory cultural norms. For John, Jesus' signs are evidence confirming his affiliation with Yahweh.

In light of these varying portrayals, it is little wonder that we have four gospels. Had the evangelists considered the work of their predecessors sufficient, there would have been little reason for them to pen their own! Because each approaches his subject from a unique angle, we are ultimately left with a complex picture (actually, it's more of a *collage*) of Jesus and his ministry. Which is the *right* one? Undoubtedly, each of them captures various aspects of the truth. For this reason we need not elevate one over the others. The church has preserved all four for good reason. Just as four walk-throughs with different brokers would ultimately enhance one's collective knowledge of a given property, so too do these divergent gospel structures ultimately enrich our collective understanding of Jesus and his ministry.

5
Jesus' Parables

THE GOOD SAMARITAN AND THE DISHONEST STEWARD

FOCUS TEXTS: LUKE 16:1–13; 10:29–37

*H*aving observed the perspectives that underlie each gospel's ministerial framework, we can now turn our attention to individual episodes that comprise Jesus' ministry, beginning with Jesus' parables. When it comes to these lessons, discovering their historical foundations can have a couple of effects. In many cases, this process can enhance the meaning of a story by sharpening and clarifying what is already there. But sometimes it can have a more transformational effect by divulging information that has been completely obscured.

We can liken these outcomes to those achieved by the process of artistic restoration. In this respect, it is helpful to think of the individual incidents from Jesus' ministry as Renaissance paintings, whose original hues, shades, and tones have been dulled by centuries of exposure to light, dirt, humidity, and other environmental menaces. Take Michelangelo's work in the Sistine Chapel, for example. For years it was simply assumed that the renowned artist had chosen to work with rather insipid and subdued colors for this particular commissioning. Only in the aftermath of one of the most sophisticated and ambitious enterprises in art conservation history were preservationists able to reveal the crisp, brilliant vibrancy of Michelangelo's frescos. In much the same way, peeling back the obscuring layers of history serves to "restore" the evangelists' "masterpieces." This process does not replace the subject in view, but by returning the work to its original condition, it enables the modern reader to perceive all the richness, depth, and nuance that inherently belong to the composition.

Occasionally, of course, the efforts of art conservators cause more of a paradigmatic shift in a given work. Their use of modern ultraviolet, infrared, and x-ray technologies enable them to perceive details on canvasses that are otherwise invisible to the naked eye. Sometimes their discoveries "beneath the surface" challenge our prevailing assumptions about the subject in view. Such is the case with Raphael's *The Baker Girl* (*La Fornarina*).

Some experts in the art world suspected that Raphael had become deeply enamored with its sitter, Margherita Luti, the daughter of a Roman baker. After all, he had immortalized her in a number of his works throughout Rome. But these suspicions were met with skepticism, especially given Raphael's very public, six-year betrothal to Maria Bibiena, the niece of his cardinal-patron. Unfortunately, Raphael never did marry. When the thirty-seven-year-old artist suddenly died in 1520, Bibiena was left with an empty promise, and Luti checked herself into the Convent of Saint Apollonia. Her portrait was only half finished.

But the story doesn't end there. In December 2000, the Associated Press reported that curators working on *The Baker Girl* discovered a detail that had been concealed since the artist's death: a square-cut, ruby-red engagement ring on the fourth finger of her left hand! It is not known who painted over the ring. Some suspect it was Giulio Romano, who eventually finished the work before selling it. Others contend it was Raphael himself, perhaps to avoid the scandal it would have caused given his relationship with Bibiena. At any rate, this detail radically recasts the subject in view. Rather than understanding *La Fornarina* as just another study in feminine form, the evidence now suggests that the baker girl was in fact Raphael's secret lover. Revealed historical premises can function similarly. Sometimes they do more than just enhance the scene; they dramatically alter our assumptions about the subject in view.

Two of Jesus' parables in the gospel of Luke exemplify these effects. In "The Good Samaritan," unpacking the historical context serves to enhance Jesus' lesson. In "The Dishonest Steward," the premises have more of a transformational impact upon our perception of the central character.

The Good Samaritan

"The Good Samaritan" is, of course, one of the most popular stories in the NT. It appears only in Luke's gospel, where it follows a discussion between a scholar of the law and Jesus. The scholar asks Jesus what he must do to inherit eternal life. Jesus turns the question back to him: "What is written in the Law? How do you read it?" The man responds that one must love God completely and love one's neighbor as oneself. Jesus approves this answer, but the scholar pursues it further: "Who is my neighbor?" In reply, Jesus addresses this parable to him:

> A man fell victim to robbers as he went down from Jerusalem to Jericho. They stripped and beat him and went off leaving him half-dead. A priest happened to be going down that road, but when he saw him, he passed by on the opposite side. Likewise a Levite came to the place, and when he saw him, he passed by on the opposite side. But a Samaritan traveler who came upon him was moved with compassion at the sight. He approached the victim, poured oil and wine over his wounds and bandaged them. Then he lifted him up on his own animal, took him to an inn and cared for him. The next day he took out two silver coins and gave them to the innkeeper with the instruction, "Take care of him. If you spend more than what I have given you, I shall repay you on my way back." (Luke 10:30–35 NAB)

Most modern readers get the point. The priest and Levite are the ones who should have rendered assistance, but they didn't. The Samaritan becomes the unlikely hero of the story. He is the one who epitomizes neighborly love.

But if we press this interpretation a little further, some of the details become unclear. Why *should* the priest and Levite be expected to stop? Why *didn't* they? More important, what makes the *Samaritan* such an improbable candidate for aiding the victim?

To appreciate the full impact of this parable, it is best to understand it from the perspective of the one to whom it was directed. When Jesus questions the scholar about the law, the man responds by quoting it. The first part of his answer (love God completely) can be found in Deut 6:5 (see also Deut 10:12; Josh 22:5). The second part (love your neighbor as yourself) occurs in Lev 19:18. Note that it is only this second part—and not the first—that the scholar seeks to clarify.

Jesus' answer demonstrates his own affinity with the law. Just two verses prior to the scholar's chosen quotation, this directive appears:

> [You shall not] stand by idly when your neighbor's life is at stake. (Lev 19:16 NAB)

The scholar would have recognized that both the priest and the Levite failed to follow this statute. But he also would have understood that this injunction applies equally to *all* Jews. One might expect the priest and the Levite—those who embody the highest degrees of holiness—to be especially obligated to comply. However, as any legal expert would have known, the guidelines surrounding priestly and Levitical purity would have created an unusual dilemma for these two characters.

In his parable, Jesus states that the victim was left "half dead." It is this detail that poses the potential problem. The Torah stipulates that contact with the dead is generally to be avoided since it made a person "unclean":

> This is the law: When a man dies in a tent, everyone who enters the tent, as well as everyone already in it, shall be unclean for seven days; likewise, every vessel that is open, or with its lid unfastened, shall be unclean. Moreover, everyone who in the open country touches a dead person, whether he was slain by the sword or died naturally, or who touches a human bone or a grave, shall be unclean for seven days. (Num 19:14–16 NAB)

Because they ministered in the temple sanctuary, priests were strictly forbidden from having contact with anything that might render them "unclean"—especially the dead. Only for the death of their immediate relatives does the Torah permit an exception (Lev 21:1–4):

> The LORD said to Moses, "Speak to Aaron's sons, the priests, and tell them: None of you shall make himself unclean for any dead person among his people, except for his nearest relatives, his mother or father, his son or daughter, his brother or his maiden sister, who is of his own family while she remains unmarried; for these he may make himself unclean." (Lev 21:1–3 NAB)

The Levites assisted the priests in the temple precincts by preparing various offerings and acting as musicians, gatekeepers, and general custodians. Because of their involvements, they, too, were required to observe the priestly standards (Num 2:47–54; 3:5–13; 8:5–26; 18:1–7; 1 Chr 23:28–31).

The scholar would have known the quandary the priest and Levite both faced. Should they maintain their ritual purity or save a man's life? Both chose cult over compassion. Most likely, the scholar would have approved. After all, they appear to regard their love for God as more important than their love for neighbor. Fortunately for the victim, the story doesn't end there. Into the breach steps a Samaritan.

Today, many people have a vague sense of the enmity between Jews and Samaritans, but few realize just how deep the divide really was. Surely the scholar knew. The long-standing rivalry between these two groups can be summarized chronologically:

circa 930 BCE Upon the death of King Solomon, the twelve tribes of the united monarchy are fractured. Ten of them, collectively known as "Israel," consolidate in the northern region and establish Samaria as their capital. The two remaining tribes, collectively known as "Judah," maintain the capital in Jerusalem. The inhabitants of Israel and Judah become the antecedents of the Samaritans and the Jews.

circa 722 BCE The forces of Assyria invade Israel and displace the majority of its citizens. The Assyrians then resettle the region with refugees from Babylon, Cuthah, Avva, Hamath, and Sepharvaim. These foreigners—and their religions—soon intermingle with the surviving Israelites. This aggregate group becomes known as the Samaritans (2 Kgs 17:24–41).

circa 589 BCE Judah loses its sovereignty when the Babylonians invade and deport its residents back to Babylon.

circa 538–445 BCE The Jews are liberated from Babylon by the Persians and are allowed to return to Judea. There, they set about restoring the temple. The Samaritans offer their assistance, but are rejected. Consequently, the Samaritans devise ways to hinder the work. The Samaritan antagonism continues as the Jews rebuild Jerusalem's walls (Ezra 4; Nehemiah 4–6).

circa 332 BCE Manasseh, the brother of the high priest, marries a Samaritan woman. Consequently, Manasseh is stripped of his priestly privileges in Jerusalem. This action causes a revolt, and a contingent of priests and Levites follows Manasseh to Samaria. There, they build a rival temple to Yahweh on Mount Gerizim and follow their own version of the Torah (*Ant.* 11.304–312).

circa 175–163 BCE Bent on Hellenizing the region, the Seleucid king Antiochus IV Epiphanes persecutes the Jews and desecrates their temple. Seeking to avoid similar treatment, the Samaritans renounce their heritage with the Jews and rename their temple the "temple of Jupiter Hellenius" (*Ant.* 12.257–263).

circa 128 BCE John Hyrcanus, the Jewish high priest, lays siege to Samaria in retribution for the Samaritan attack on Marissa, a colony of Jews. He forces the Samaritans into famine, demolishes their city, and reduces the Gerizim temple to rubble (*Ant.* 13.275–281).

circa 6–9 CE During the Passover festival, a group of Samaritans enters the Jerusalem temple after midnight and scatters dead men's bones throughout its sanctuary. Henceforth, Jews deny temple access to all Samaritans (*Ant.* 18.29–30).

The animosity between the Jews and the Samaritans continued well into the first century. The gospel of John reports that the Jews refused to use anything in common with the Samaritans (John 4:9). In fact, one rabbinic commentator in the Mishnah (a collection of sixty-three legal tractates compiled around 200 CE that expand, apply, and clarify various points of Jewish law) likened eating the bread of a Samaritan to eating the flesh of swine (*m. Seb.* 8:10)! Even Jesus experiences some of the fallout from this conflict. According to Luke, Jesus is prevented from entering a Samaritan village on his way to Jerusalem. So offended are Jesus' disciples that they seek to call down fire from heaven to annihilate the town (Luke 9:51–56). Ironically—or not—this incident occurs shortly before the scholar's question.

The scholar of the law likely shared the disciples' disdain for the Samaritans. In many respects, he probably considered them to be inferior even to the Gentiles. Whereas the Gentiles had never known God, the Samaritans once had. Because they abandoned the *true* worship of Yahweh to pursue foreign marriages and alien gods, the Samaritans were worse than nonbelievers. They were apostates!

In light of this background, the scholar was astonished, no doubt, by the Samaritan's role in the parable. Here was an individual who had clearly forsaken the cult—yet *he* was showing compassion; *he* was the hero. Jesus wanted the scholar to imitate a *Samaritan!*

These restorative premises reveal the ingenious double meaning behind Jesus' lesson. The parable does more than simply teach the scholar about loving his *neighbor*—the subject of his initial inquiry. It also challenges the scholar's assumptions about loving *God*—that portion of his answer that he mistakenly presumed to understand.

Obviously, the subtle, double meaning of "The Good Samaritan" has become somewhat blurred over the two millennia since Luke first penned it. Nevertheless, thanks to clarification of the historical context, Luke's characters—like Michelangelo's in the Sistine chapel—can reemerge in all of their variegated complexity. Their restored details serve primarily to enhance the point of the parable. But as we shall see in the case of "The Dishonest Steward," sometimes premises can have a more dramatic, even transformational effect upon the subject in view.

The Dishonest Steward

The parable of the dishonest steward is one of the most enigmatic passages in the NT. Jesus describes it accordingly:

> A rich man had a steward who was reported to him for squandering his property. He summoned him and said, "What is this I hear about you? Prepare a full account of your stewardship, because you can no longer be my steward." The steward said to himself, "What shall I do, now that my master is taking the position of steward away from me? I am not strong enough to dig and I am ashamed to beg. I know what I shall do so that, when I am removed from the stewardship, they may welcome me into their homes." He called in his master's debtors one by one. To the first he said, "How much do you owe my master?" He replied, "One hundred measures of olive oil." He said to him, "Here is your promissory note. Sit down and quickly write one for fifty." Then to another he said, "And you, how much do you owe?" He replied, "One hundred kors of wheat." He said to him, "Here is your promissory note; write one for eighty." And the master commended that dishonest steward for acting prudently. (Luke 16:1–8 NAB)

In its present form, this parable appears to be self-contradictory. The steward stands accused of mismanaging his master's assets. Because of this charge, his master sets about relieving him from his duty. Realizing that his future is in jeopardy, the steward has his master's debtors rewrite their promissory notes. That this action places the steward in the good graces of the borrowers is completely understandable. After all, their sums have been reduced by twenty to fifty percent. What baffles many readers is the reaction of the master. He actually *praises* the steward for his behavior! The discrepancy, of course, is this: On the one hand, the master seeks to dismiss his steward because he has squandered the master's resources; on the other, he extols him for ostensibly the same reason!

To complicate the matter further, Jesus then upholds the steward as a role model for his disciples:

> For the children of this world are more prudent in dealing with their own generation than are the children of light. I tell you, make friends for yourselves with dishonest wealth, so that when it fails, you will be welcomed into eternal dwellings. (16:8–9 NAB)

On the face of it, Jesus' words seem to permit—and even to encourage—self-promotion by embezzlement! Is it possible that Jesus condoned such behavior? That hardly seems likely. In fact, this interpretation not only fails to square with Jesus' portrayal throughout the NT, it blatantly contradicts his teaching that immediately follows:

> The person who is trustworthy in very small matters is also trustworthy in great ones; and the person who is dishonest in very small matters is also dishonest in great ones. If, therefore, you are not trustworthy with worldly wealth, who will trust you with true wealth? If you are not trustworthy with what belongs to another, who will give you what is yours? (16:10–12 NAB)

What, then, is the point of this parable? Like *The Baker Girl,* "The Dishonest Steward" is missing a key detail that transforms its subject. Unlike Raphael's work, there is no evidence that this detail was deliberately excised from Luke's text. Nonetheless it remains just "under the surface." Its absence is likely the result of Luke's assumptions about his audience. That which eludes us moderns would have been understood naturally by his first-century readers.

In the ancient Greco-Roman world, when a master entrusted his financial affairs to a manager, that manager earned his commission from the various transactions of the estate. His commission would be a percentage of the assets involved, depending on the agreements he himself had brokered. Although the Torah explicitly forbids Jews from charging the poor (Exod 22:24) or each other (Lev 25:36–37) interest, it does allow them to receive it from the Gentiles (Deut 23:20–21). Of course, Luke is writing primarily to a Gentile audience, where the prohibitions against usury would have been less stringent.

When the steward in Jesus' parable realizes his employment is about to be terminated, he visits his master's associates and reduces their debts by the percentage of his commission. In light of his impending future, the steward is willing to forgo what is rightfully his—his commission—in order to befriend those with the means to assist him.

This premise explains why the master responds to the steward's plan with admiration rather than anger. The steward did not deduct from his master's capital, but from his own. It also explains Jesus' use of the steward as a model of discipleship. Jesus charges his followers to use their resources to make friends, so that "when it fails," they will be "welcomed into eternal dwellings."

To explain Jesus' injunction more concretely, it is helpful to have a working knowledge of Luke's theology. The "failure" that Jesus describes is not a cessation of cash flow, but the inevitable condition that renders all wealth useless: death (so Luke 12:16–21). Luke's Jesus thus enjoins his disciples to use their earthly resources in this life to procure their status in the next. How? Like the steward, the disciple must seek to cull the favor of those who hold sway in the kingdom. In the divine economy, however, it is not the rich, but the poor who enjoy this privilege:

> Blessed are you who are poor, for the kingdom of God is yours. (Luke 6:20 NAB)

The marginalized, then, are the "debtors" whose friendship now becomes imperative. Thus, those who are wise will, in light of their unavoidable fates, voluntarily surrender that which is rightfully theirs (their wages, etc.) in order to aid the destitute. Only such prudent use of "worldly" wealth can result in "true" reward. Luke's Jesus promotes this type of behavior—and its eternal benefits—not only here, but throughout this gospel (e.g., 12:33; 16:25; 18:22, 29–30).

To recap, then, the history behind the parable of "The Good Samaritan," like the restoration work on Michelangelo's figures, serves primarily to enhance its significance. The laws governing priests and Levites and the long-standing hostilities between Jews and Samaritans sharpen the motivations of these characters. Framed as it is by the scholar's question, this parable speaks not only to the love of neighbor, but to the love of God as well.

Like the recovered ring on *The Baker Girl,* the premises behind "The Dishonest Steward" have a more transformational effect. As it turns out, the steward in question is not nearly as dishonest as he is shrewd. By forgoing his commission in order to endear himself to the business partners, the clever steward assures himself a secure future. It is this type of resourcefulness that Jesus seeks to cultivate among his disciples. By relinquishing what is theirs, they, too, can curry the favor of the poor and thus procure for themselves a place in God's kingdom.

6

Jesus' Teachings

THE BREAD OF LIFE DISCOURSE

FOCUS TEXT: JOHN 6:25–71

A s perplexing as Jesus' parables can be, sometimes his teachings are even more so. Take, for instance, Jesus' "Bread of Life Discourse" in the gospel of John. The first part of chapter 6 sets the stage. Jesus supernaturally multiplies five loaves and two fish to feed a crowd of five thousand. The remaining fragments fill twelve baskets. The crowd is so impressed with Jesus' miracle that they declare him to be "the prophet" (like Moses) and set about installing him as king (like David). Jesus resists their overtures and departs instead for Capernaum. Once the people discover that Jesus has gone, they pursue and eventually locate him there. It is at that point that Jesus launches into his teaching.

The discourse begins with an exchange between Jesus and his followers. He accuses them of being motivated by hunger rather than true faith and enjoins them to believe in him. They request a "sign" along the lines of manna, the so-called bread from heaven their ancestors ate in the desert. They want Jesus to give them this bread "always." (Evidently Jesus was correct—they *were* prompted by their appetites!) Jesus then explains to them the difference between the "bread from heaven" that God provided their forefathers and the "bread from heaven" he now offers:

> I am the bread of life. Your ancestors ate the manna in the desert, but they died; this is the bread that comes down from heaven so that one may eat it and not die. I am the living bread that came down from

heaven; whoever eats this bread will live forever; and the bread that I will give is my flesh for the life of the world. (John 6:48–51 NAB)

These words cause a considerable dispute among Jesus' listeners, who wonder how he can give them his flesh to eat. Jesus thus elaborates:

Amen, amen, I say to you, unless you eat the flesh of the Son of Man and drink his blood, you do not have life within you. Whoever eats my flesh and drinks my blood has eternal life, and I will raise him on the last day. For my flesh is true food, and my blood is true drink. Whoever eats my flesh and drinks my blood remains in me and I in him. Just as the living Father sent me and I have life because of the Father, so also the one who feeds on me will have life because of me. This is the bread that came down from heaven. Unlike your ancestors who ate and still died, whoever eats this bread will live forever. (6:53–58 NAB)

In response to these words, those assembled conclude, "This is a hard saying; who can accept it?" (6:60 NAB). Consequently,

Many [of] his disciples returned to their former way of life and no longer accompanied him. Jesus then said to the Twelve, "Do you also want to leave?" Simon Peter answered him, "Master, to whom shall we go? You have the words of eternal life. We have come to believe and are convinced that you are the Holy One of God." (6:66–69 NAB)

Jesus' "Bread of Life Discourse" thus marks a significant turning point in John's gospel. At its onset, thousands of devotees seek after Jesus. By its conclusion, only twelve or so remain. Why do the multitudes, who were just convinced of Jesus' messianic potential, now part his company? What do they find so troubling about Jesus' declaration?

Many modern readers would take these to be rhetorical questions. Their answer appears to be obvious. Jesus' followers leave because of what he is insinuating. The prospect of eating human flesh and drinking human blood conjures up notions of savage cannibals or ghoulish vampires, not faith-filled Christians. But Jesus' insistence that his flesh is "true food" and that his blood is "true drink" suggests few interpretative options. Furthermore, his allegation that one's eternal destiny is predicated upon this act leaves his audience with no viable alternative. (In this respect, the incident appears to

bear a close resemblance to an episode of *Fear Factor:* if the participants want the big payoff, they've got to be willing to swallow just
about anything.) The common assumption, therefore, is that the
crowds depart because they "chickened out." They simply consider
Jesus' proposal too grotesque.

This assumption, however, fails to grasp the more likely reason
the vast majority abandons him. John signals another reason at the
conclusion of Jesus' speech, just before their withdrawal:

> These things he said while teaching in the synagogue in Capernaum.
> (6:59 NAB)

As is evidenced by this notation and other references throughout the discourse, Jesus is addressing a group of Jews. As such, they
knew what many modern readers are completely unaware of. They
knew what the Torah stipulates about blood:

> Every creature that lives shall be yours to eat; as with the green grasses,
> I give you all these. You must not, however, eat flesh with its life-blood
> in it. (Gen 9:3–4 NJPS)

> It is a law for all time throughout the ages, in all your settlements: you
> must not eat any fat or any blood. (Lev 3:17 NJPS)

> And you must not consume any blood, either of bird or of animal, in
> any of your settlements. Anyone who eats blood shall be cut off from
> among his kin. (Lev 7:26–27 NJPS)

> Therefore I say to the Israelite people: No person among you shall par-
> take of blood, nor shall the stranger who resides among you partake of
> blood. (Lev 17:12 NJPS)

> For the life of all flesh—its blood is its life. Therefore I say to the Isra-
> elite people: You shall not partake of the blood of any flesh, for the life
> of all flesh is its blood. Anyone who partakes of it shall be cut off. (Lev
> 17:14 NJPS)

> You shall not eat anything with its blood. (Lev 19:26 NJPS)

> But whenever you desire, you may slaughter and eat meat in any of
> your settlements. . . . But you must not partake of the blood; you shall
> pour it out on the ground like water. (Deut 12:15–16 NJPS)

But make sure that you do not partake of the blood; for the blood is the life, and you must not consume the life with the flesh. You must not partake of it; you must pour it out on the ground like water: you must not partake of it, in order that it may go will with you and with your descendants to come. (Deut 12:23–25 NJPS)

Eat [the consecrated meat] in your settlements, the unclean among you no less than the clean, just like the gazelle and the deer. Only you must not partake of its blood; you shall pour it out on the ground like water. (Deut 15:22–23 NJPS)

According to the Torah, the Jews (and Gentiles) are strictly forbidden from consuming blood. As the nine passages above demonstrate, this is hardly an inconspicuous command. Few prohibitions appear more frequently. (The injunction against idolatry may be the only exception.) Nor can its violation be considered a minor offense. Its punishment entails being "cut off from among the people."

This phrase, "cut off from among the people," can be interpreted in a couple of different ways. It can refer to a sort of excommunication, whereby an individual would be ostracized from the community of faith. In light of its original setting, this punishment would have had more than just spiritual implications. When the Hebrews first received these commands, they were reportedly still wandering in the desert. In this hostile environment, expulsion from the group meant separation from vital resources. Under these circumstances, long-term survival would have been extremely difficult.

The phrase can also be interpreted more literally. In this sense, to be "cut off from among the people" denotes complete extermination. Although the Torah does not specify which of these two meanings is intended, it leans closer to the second. The later rabbis confirm this assessment in the Mishnah. There, the consumption of blood is listed as one of the thirty-six offenses that merit death if committed deliberately (*m. Ker.* 1:1).

Against this background, the decision of the masses to return to their former ways of life makes perfect sense. Jesus' teaching appears to be in direct opposition to God's law, and anyone who acts on it would face dire consequences. We can surmise, therefore, that the people disperse because of their loyalty to God, their fear of punishment, or (most likely) for both of these reasons.

These considerations, of course, beg the question of Jesus' intent. Why would he who claims to be the "Son of God" so blatantly contradict his Father?

Some have speculated that perhaps Jesus felt the need to rebel against his parent as most children do from time to time. While this may be true of our experience, this suggestion overlooks the fact that Jesus' obedience to God—even unto death—is repeatedly affirmed throughout the NT (e.g., Mark 14:36; Matt 26:36; Luke 22:42; Rom 5:19; Phil 2:5–11; Heb 5:7–9). Furthermore, the great lengths John goes to in order to demonstrate the intimate relationship between Jesus and Yahweh (see ch. 4) render this proposal even more improbable.

Others submit that Jesus was testing his followers. Perhaps he wanted to see who *really* had faith in him? This possibility is a little more intriguing, but still problematic. After all, who would "pass" this test? As they are recorded in the Torah, virtually all of the blood prohibition passages are direct quotations from the mouth of God. Presumably, God had given these laws (among others) to his people in order to establish his expectations of them. Although they were not always successful, the Jews endeavored to live by these rules as a sign of their fidelity to God. Therefore, the only ones who would qualify as Jesus' disciples would be those who didn't know or didn't care about God's expressed wishes. As John's context makes clear, the former case doesn't apply. The assembled Jews demonstrate that they are well versed in the Hebrew Scriptures. As for the alternative, it seems incredible—especially given the theology of John's gospel—that Jesus would want to gather around him those with no regard for his Father's words.

So if Jesus wasn't rebelling against his parent or testing his disciples' faith, what *was* he doing? The key to Jesus' intent lies with the prohibitions themselves. In other words, in order to understand why Jesus commanded his followers to eat his flesh and drink his blood, one has to know why such a practice was barred in the first place.

As Lev 17:14 explains, "the life of every living body is its blood" (NAB). The ancients, of course, lacked access to the sophisticated medical technology of today. They couldn't detect brain waves or record heart rhythms. Rather, their experience taught them that blood contained life. Whether it was an animal caught in the hunt or a human wounded in battle, as a body lost its blood, so it lost its life.

Because blood was considered the seat of life, to consume another's blood was to intermingle their existence. Thus, the lad who drinks the blood of a goat becomes, in effect, "goat-boy"—part goat, part boy. As the blood of the goat is taken in, so too is its life. Theoretically, such an act would allow the goat to abide within the boy's body.

Throughout the Torah, there are ordinances that generally prohibit the Israelites from intermingling. They are forbidden, for example, from crossbreeding different species of animals (Lev 19:19), sowing different kinds of seed in the same field (Deut 22:9), wearing clothes of blended materials (Deut 22:11), and even harnessing an ox together with an ass (Deut 22:10). In light of these restrictions, the mingling of life becomes the ultimate taboo. Whereas the others disrupt the world outside of the individual, this one alters individuals themselves.

Yet it is for precisely this reason that Jesus enjoins his followers to eat his flesh and drink his blood. According to the gospel of John, Jesus possesses eternal life. Assuming that his life is in his blood, then the only way for his followers to share in this life is to consume his blood. In this way, Jesus' divine life mingles with theirs, and they have life because of him. This premise now lends considerable clarity to Jesus' statement above:

> Unless you eat the flesh of the Son of Man and drink his blood, you do not have life within you. Whoever eats my flesh and drinks my blood has eternal life, and I will raise him on the last day. . . . Whoever eats my flesh and drinks my blood remains in me and I in him. Just as the living Father sent me and I have life because of the Father, so also the one who feeds on me will have life because of me. (6:53–57 NAB)

Jesus is not so much breaking God's law as he is fulfilling it. He becomes the one exception to the rule—the one instance where intermingling is not only permissible, but absolutely crucial for one's eternal preservation.

Even given this explanation, Jesus' disciples must have found themselves facing a difficult dilemma. To appreciate their situation, consider this modern scenario: Suppose you're near the end of a three-year public-health residency under a physician in a developing country. One day, following your own routine physical, she announces some troubling news. You've acquired a rare blood disease, the symptoms of which you've been ignoring or have yet to manifest. She tells you that without an immediate blood transfusion, you will soon experience shock, coma, and death. Without delay, she arranges for the transfusion by setting up two cots—one for you, one for her. Every fiber in your being recognizes the breech in protocol. Her blood has not been properly screened for potentially deadly pathogens such as malaria, syphilis, hepatitis B, or HIV. You're not even certain she has a compatible blood type! And yet, you've developed nothing but respect and esteem for this physician over the past three years. Her judgment has always been sound. If she is correct, forgoing the transfusion could be equally dangerous. What would you do? The disciples, of course, put their trust in Jesus. Difficult as it is, they are willing to accept his invitation.

Given the necessity of this act, it might seem strange that John records not a single instance of Jesus' disciples actually eating his flesh or drinking his blood. On the other hand, it would be equally strange if he did! Are we to conclude, therefore, that the disciples' eternal security remained in jeopardy? Jesus' assurance elsewhere in this gospel (e.g., 14:1–3) indicates otherwise. But if the disciples didn't partake of his flesh and blood, then how did they come to share in his life?

Jesus' self-identification as the "bread of life" and the "bread that came down from heaven" establishes a relationship between himself and bread. John, therefore, seems to assume what the other evangelists make explicit. Namely, that Jesus' flesh and blood can somehow be represented in bread and wine:

> And as they were eating, he took bread, and blessed, and broke it, and gave it to them, and said, "Take; this is my body." And he took a cup, and when he had given thanks he gave it to them, and they all drank of it. And he said to them, "This is my blood of the covenant, which is poured out for many." (Mark 14:22–24 RSV//Matt 26:26–28//Luke 22:17–20)

The tradition of Christians gathering together over bread and wine to remember Jesus and "to give thanks" (in Greek, *eucharistein*) became one of the earliest and most prominent practices of the church. In fact, even before the gospels were written, the Apostle Paul recognized its signification:

The cup of blessing which we bless, is it not a participation in the blood of Christ? The bread which we break, is it not a participation in the body of Christ? (1 Cor 10:16 RSV)

Of course, the celebration of Communion, Eucharist, or the Lord's Supper is actively practiced by most Christian faiths today. Although they disagree over the details, most mainline denominations acknowledge as least some degree of correspondence between Jesus' presence and the elements of bread and wine. Accordingly, the power of this sacrament to affect a change in the life of the believer is widely maintained.

7

Jesus' Works

THE CURSING OF THE FIG TREE AND
THE CLEANSING OF THE TEMPLE

FOCUS TEXTS: MARK 11:12–21; MATTHEW 21:12–22

*H*aving examined the premises behind some of Jesus' parables and teachings, we can now round out our survey of his public ministry with a look at Jesus' actions. Of course, most of Jesus' recorded deeds are miraculous in nature. He multiplies food and stills storms, casts out demons and heals the sick. He even walks on water and raises the dead. But few of Jesus' exploits are as peculiar or as controversial as the pair that he performs at the very conclusion of his public ministry: Jesus curses a fig tree and "cleanses" the temple. Because Mark and Matthew are the only evangelists to include both of these events, we shall concentrate primarily upon their accounts, and compare Luke and John where relevant. We'll begin with Mark's version of these incidents, since his gospel (ca. 70 CE) chronologically precedes Matthew's (ca. 85 CE).

Mark's Version

According to Mark, Jesus had triumphantly entered Jerusalem several days before he would celebrate his last Passover meal, the Last Supper, with his disciples. Immediately following his arrival, Jesus

> went into the temple area. He looked around at everything and, since it was already late, went out to Bethany with the Twelve. (Mark 11:11 NAB)

It is what Jesus does the ensuing day that proves so bewildering:

> The next day as they were leaving Bethany he was hungry. Seeing from a distance a fig tree in leaf, he went over to see if he could find anything on it. When he reached it he found nothing but leaves; it was not the time for figs. And he said to it in reply, "May no one ever eat of your fruit again!" And his disciples heard it. (11:12–14 NAB)

Jesus and his disciples proceed on to Jerusalem and then return to Bethany that evening. The next day,

> early in the morning, as they were walking along, they saw the fig tree withered to its roots. Peter remembered and said to him, "Rabbi, look! The fig tree that you cursed has withered." (11:20–21 NAB)

When most modern readers encounter this story, they are rightly troubled by Jesus' behavior. His deliberate destruction of the tree appears to be motivated by nothing more than his own, frustrated hunger. Jesus' wrath seems entirely unjustified. Why ruin an innocent and otherwise healthy plant? After all, it wasn't even the season for figs!

This disturbing incident is so uncharacteristic of Jesus it is hardly surprising that neither Luke nor John mention it. It is quite possible, however, that Luke, who wrote later than Mark, used it as the basis for a similar—but decidedly more dignified—parable:

> There once was a person who had a fig tree planted in his orchard, and when he came in search of fruit on it but found none, he said to the gardener, "For three years now I have come in search of fruit on this fig tree but have found none. (So) cut it down. Why should it exhaust the soil?" He said to him in reply, "Sir, leave it for this year also, and I shall cultivate the ground around it and fertilize it; it may bear fruit in the future. If not you can cut it down." (Luke 13:6–9 NAB)

In Luke's gospel, this parable is found amidst lessons on judgment and repentance (so Luke 13:1–5). In this setting, the gardener's mercy and patient cultivation that affords the barren fig tree a final opportunity to yield fruit (or suffer the consequences) reflects the Lord's mercy and patient cultivation that affords the sinner a final opportunity to yield a productive life or suffer the consequences.

Ironically, Luke's version of the barren fig tree emphasizes the very *opposite* quality of Mark's account. In Luke, the gardener (Jesus) demonstrates considerable compassion and forbearance toward the fig tree. In Mark, Jesus appears to condemn it prematurely! But if Luke is unwilling to accept this negative portrayal of Jesus, why does Mark permit it? The answer lies with the premises that bear upon this scene.

To someone with a local knowledge of fig trees, certain aspects of Jesus' behavior would not have seemed so bizarre. According to Pliny the Elder (a Roman scholar and natural historian who lived from 23 to 79 CE), the fig tree is different from most other trees in one important respect: Its fruit actually begins to form *before* its leaves, in early spring (*Nat.* 16.49). As the leaves develop later in the spring, the fruit continues to grow. Typically, figs are fully ripe and ready for harvest between late May and June.

According to Mark, Jesus arrives at the fig tree just before Passover. This would put him there early to mid-April—at least a month prior to harvest time. Presumably, Jesus knew when figs would have been ripe. What, then, was he looking for? Unripe fruit? Certainly there should have been some, given the fact that the tree was full of leaves. But one could hardly expect Jesus to satisfy his appetite with inedible, immature figs.

Rather, Jesus was most likely looking for the "first" or "early figs." This type of fig is mentioned several times in the Hebrew Bible, where it is referred to as *bikkura* (from the root *bkr*, a verb meaning "to come forth early or first"). The Greek names convey its tendency more colorfully. It is referred to variously as "the scout" *(skopos)* and "the one that runs ahead" *(prodromos)*. Ostensibly, this fig is not a distinct species or variety, but refers to individual members that, for whatever reason, are ready before the rest. According to the OT, the early figs are somewhat rare and are considered far superior in taste to those that ripen later.

As a lifelong native of Palestine, Jesus' knowledge of the growing season can be assumed. Even though it is not yet harvest time, Jesus approaches the leafy fig tree in search of the succulent, early figs. Despite promising external appearances, they are nowhere to be found. Thus, Jesus' disappointment is understandable. His reaction, however, still seems strange. Why does Jesus *curse* the tree?

Mark signals his comprehension of this event through his inter-calation, or "sandwiching," of the narrative. In other words, Mark deliberately alternates between two different episodes in order to interpret one in light of the other. (For Mark's use of this technique elsewhere, see 3:20–35; 5:21–43; 14:53–72.) As noted above, Mark prefaces the fig tree scene with Jesus' visit to the temple (11:11). After Jesus curses the tree, he returns to the temple, where his anger continues to flair:

> And on entering the temple area he began to drive out those selling and buying there. He overturned the tables of the money changers and the seats of those who were selling doves. He did not permit anyone to carry anything through the temple area. Then he taught them saying, "Is it not written: 'My house shall be called a house of prayer for all peoples'? But you have made it a den of thieves." (11:15–17 NAB)

Jesus leaves Jerusalem that evening (11:19), encounters the withered fig tree the following morning (11:20–21), and then returns once again to the temple area (11:27). Mark's arrangement of this section corresponds to the following pattern:

Literary Structure of Mark 11:11–27	
A	Jesus enters the *temple* area. (11:11)
B	Jesus curses the *fig tree*. (11:12–14)
A	Jesus drives out the merchants in the *temple*. (11:15–19)
B	The *fig tree* is withered. (11:20–21)
A	Jesus returns to the *temple*. (11:27)

Evidently, Mark seeks to explain the cursing of the fig tree in light of Jesus' actions in the temple. But what do figs have to do with the temple? The relationship would have been fairly obvious to Mark's original audience.

It was noted above that the OT portrays the early figs as delicacies. They were so prized, in fact, that God repeatedly compares his faithful to them:

> When I found Israel, it was like finding grapes in the desert; when I saw your fathers, it was like seeing the early fruit on the fig tree. (Hos 9:10 NIV)

The LORD showed me two baskets of figs placed before the temple. . . . One basket contained excellent figs, the early-ripening kind. But the other basket contained very bad figs, so bad they could not be eaten. . . . Thereupon this word of the LORD came to me: . . . Like these good figs, even so will I regard with favor Judah's exiles. . . . I will look after them for their good, and bring them back to this land. . . . I will give them a heart with which to understand that I am the LORD. They shall be my people and I will be their God, for they shall return to me with their whole heart. (Jer 24:1–7 NAB)

Alas! I am as when the fruit is gathered, as when the vines have been gleaned; there is no cluster to eat, no early fig that I crave. The faithful are gone from the earth, among men the upright are no more! (Mic 7:1–2 NAB)

If the early figs symbolize fidelity, then the link between Jesus' cursing of the fig tree and his ruckus in the temple begins to make sense. From a distance, the leafy tree showed promise of the desirable, early figs. However, the external indicators were misleading. The tree was barren. In much the same way, the temple compound boasted a grand exterior. (According to Mark 13:1, even Jesus' disciples are impressed.) But the temple personnel had ceased to be the "early figs," or the faithful individuals for whom God yearned. Therefore, Mark understands Jesus' demonstration in the temple not as a *cleansing*, or an attempt to reform the religious institution, as is commonly presumed, but as a *curse* upon the temple, with the implication that it, like the fig tree, will soon wither and die. Jesus predicts as much in Mark 13:1–2//Matt 24:1–2//Luke 21:5–6.

Historically, of course, this is precisely what happened. Around 70 CE, the Romans laid siege to the city of Jerusalem and burnt the temple to the ground. It has not been rebuilt since. Although scholars disagree over the exact dating for the composition of Mark's gospel, most judge it to have been written very close to this period. Assuming they are correct, Mark evidently intended the fig tree/ temple episode to serve as an explanation of this tragedy. In other words, while Mark's original audience would have known that the temple was endangered by the Romans, Mark places the underlying reason for its demise back upon the Jews. (In fact, in *J.W.* 6.5.4

Josephus takes a similar tack.) Ultimately, it is the inability of the temple cult to produce "good fruit" that prompts Mark's Jesus to foreshadow its fate.

If the preceding assessment is accurate, then one question still remains. What was wrong with the temple establishment? In other words, how, specifically, was it unfaithful to God? The answer—or at least some facet of it—must be related to Jesus' disturbance there. On the basis of his actions and words, at least three possibilities present themselves.

One option, perhaps the most radical, is that Jesus objected to the entire sacrificial system that had become an integral part of temple operations. Jews of the time were required to present offerings for a variety of purposes, including atonement, purification, thanksgiving, etc. Jesus' disruption of the means by which such sacrifices were made appears to signal his opposition to the practices themselves. But as reasonable as this explanation seems, there is little evidence in Mark's gospel to corroborate it. At one point, Mark's Jesus does agree with a Jewish scribe about the love of God and neighbor being "worth more than all burnt offerings and sacrifices" (Mark 12:33 NAB). Nevertheless, he also directs a man he has healed of leprosy to offer the appropriate oblation before the priests (1:44). If Mark's Jesus truly seeks to end activities like money changing and dove selling—activities which are fully sanctioned by the Mosaic law (see Exod 30:11–16, Lev 12:6–8; 14:22; 15:14, 29)—one would expect him to espouse this notion elsewhere.

Another possibility is that Jesus sought to criminally indict those running the temple—the chief priests and their associates. That he considers them corrupt is indicated by his comparison of the temple to a "den of thieves." In its original context, this phrase was used as part of an accusation against Jews who were found guilty of theft, murder, adultery, perjury, and idolatry (Jer 7:11). Because of their crimes, God pledged to destroy their temple, which occurred when the Babylonians invaded in 589 BCE. The temple leadership is evidently offended by Jesus' protest—they immediately seek a way to put him to death (Mark 11:18). Furthermore, in the verses to follow, they challenge Jesus' authority (11:27–33) and are murderously portrayed in his parable of the Wicked Tenants (12:1–12). But as promising as it seems, this explanation does not fully account for Jesus' spectacle in the temple. At no point are the chief priests or other leaders the direct targets of Jesus' fury. Rather, Jesus hinders only those doing commerce, the Passover pilgrims and their vendors.

If Jesus' condemnation of the temple can be attributed neither to its sacrificial system nor its leadership *per se,* what prompted it? A third option can be proposed on the basis of certain presumptions of Mark's first-century audience. One such premise assumes familiarity with the Jerusalem temple itself.

The temple was an enormous complex, some five hundred yards (450 meters) long and 330 yards (300 meters) wide, situated on Mount Moriah. According to Josephus, it had four courts, each one somewhat contained within the other to demarcate successive degrees of purity. The expansive outer court was the Court of the Gentiles, where virtually everyone was allowed. The next was the Court of the Women, which was open to all Jews and their wives (except those in states of defilement). The third was the Court of the Men, reserved for Jewish males who were clean and purified. The fourth was the Court of the Priests, which could be accessed only by priests in their proper garments. The sanctuary, into which only the high priests were permitted, was located within this innermost court (*Ag. Ap.* 2.8.103–105).

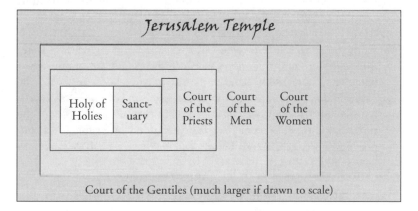

Mark's description of Jesus entering "the temple" suggests that he was in the outer court, or the Court of the Gentiles. Most likely, this is where the merchants were located. Not only does Jesus expel them from this precinct, he allows no one to carry anything through it. A prohibition against carrying vessels already existed for the *interior regions* of the temple (*Ag. Ap.* 2.8.106). Evidently, Jesus sought to extend it to the *outer court* as well.

In doing all these things, Jesus declares that God's house should be a house of prayer "for all peoples" (lit. "for all the Gentiles"). He borrows this phrase from Isa 56:7. In its fuller context, this passage envisions the day when God's temple will be open to all:

> Thus says the LORD: Observe what is right, do what is just; for my salvation is about to come, my justice, about to be revealed. . . . Let not the foreigner say, when he would join himself to the LORD, "The LORD will surely exclude me from his people"; . . . the foreigners who join themselves to the LORD, ministering to him, loving the name of the LORD, and becoming his servants—. . . them I will bring to my holy mountain and make joyful in my house of prayer; their holocausts and sacrifices will be acceptable on my altar, For my house shall be called a house of prayer for all peoples. Thus says the Lord GOD, who gathers the dispersed of Israel: Others will I gather to him besides those already gathered. (Isa 56:1, 3, 6–8 NAB)

This expectation, that the temple would become an inclusive center of worship, even for the Gentiles, corresponds to its original purpose. Solomon had stipulated as much during his invocation at the temple's dedication:

> To the foreigner, likewise, who is not of your people Israel, but comes from a distant land to honor you (since men will learn of your great name and your mighty hand and your outstretched arm), when he comes and prays toward this temple, listen from your heavenly dwelling. Do all that the foreigner asks of you, that all the peoples of the earth may know your name, may fear you as do your people Israel, and may acknowledge that this temple which I have built is dedicated to your honor. (1 Kgs 8:41–43 NAB)

The business activities in the Court of the Gentiles were not conducive to prayer. Jesus sets about rectifying this problem. He then labels the Jewish leaders "thieves," presumably because they are the ones who permit (and profit from) the commercial exploitation of the outer court. By trampling upon the rights of the Gentiles— the very group Mark's Jesus seeks to embrace (so ch. 4)—the religious rulers prevent the temple from becoming what it was created to be and thus demonstrate their infidelity to God's design. For these reasons (and others), Jesus judges the temple establishment "barren" and signals its downfall.

To recap, Mark presents Jesus' cursing of the fig tree not as a capricious act triggered by his ungratified appetite, but as a representation of God's judgment upon the temple and its leadership. In addition to their other crimes, the chief priests and their cohorts have proven themselves unfaithful to God by compromising the Court of the Gentiles. Thus, although the temple seems grand and promising in its appearance (like the leafy tree), its custodians are devoid of fidelity (without early figs) and are therefore accursed. As the withered fig tree illustrates, the collapse of this establishment is only a matter of time.

Of course, not all of the evangelists register this scene the same way that Mark does. Before turning to Matthew's version, we can touch briefly upon the temple episode as Luke and John have it.

In Luke's gospel, Jesus casts out only the sellers, and they alone are accused of being "thieves" (Luke 19:45–46). Luke's Jesus, therefore, appears to be provoked more by the corrupt transactions in the temple than the ritual defilement of it. His behavior reflects ethical, rather than cultic, concerns.

John's account is more dramatic. When Jesus enters the temple, he finds not only dove sellers and money changers, but merchants trading in sheep and oxen as well. The precincts had become a veritable livestock emporium! Thus, John's Jesus fashions a whip out of cords and proceeds to drive out both the vendors and their animals. He pours out coins and overturns tables, all the while declaring, "Stop making my Father's house a marketplace!" (John 2:13–16 NAB). Despite the extent of the trafficking involved, John's Jesus is determined to uphold the dignity appropriate to God's temple. Such is his zeal for his Father's house.

In the absence of the fig tree episode, both Luke and John portray Jesus as cleansing, rather than cursing, the temple. He redresses the wrongs being done there in the hopes of initiating reform. The remaining evangelist, Matthew, does include the fig tree episode. But as we shall see, its relationship to Jesus' demonstration in the temple is more ambiguous in Matthew's account.

Matthew's Version

Like Mark, Matthew places the fig tree incident adjacent to Jesus' appearance in the temple. But this evangelist appears to understand these two events in an entirely different way. In Matthew's version, Jesus doesn't encounter the fig tree first. Rather, following his triumphal entry into Jerusalem, he proceeds immediately to the temple and begins his demonstration against it. At this point, most of the narrative in Matthew's gospel is identical to Mark's. However, a fairly glaring difference appears at its conclusion. After Jesus' outburst,

> the blind and the lame came to him in temple, and he healed them. But when the chief priests and the scribes saw the wonderful things that he did, and the children crying out in the temple, "Hosanna to the Son of David!" they were indignant; and they said to him, "Do you hear what these are saying?" And Jesus said to them, "Yes; have you never read, 'Out of the mouth of babes and sucklings thou hast brought perfect praise'?" And leaving them, he went out of the city to Bethany and lodged there. (Matt 21:14–17 RSV)

That Jesus would heal the blind and the lame and that infants would declare his praise after he had just banished everyone else from the temple strikes many readers as odd. What is the meaning of this scene? Matthew's original audience probably would have caught on. Each of these details hinges upon Jesus' identity as the "new David." According to the OT, when David was first made king, he and his men

> went to Jerusalem against the Jebusites, the inhabitants of the land, who said to David, "You will not come in here, but the blind and the lame will ward you off"—thinking, "David cannot come in here." Nevertheless David took the stronghold of Zion, that is, the city of David. And David said on that day, "Whoever would smite the Jebusites, let him get up the water shaft to attack the lame and the blind, who are hated by David's soul." Therefore it is said, "The blind and the lame shall not come into the house." (2 Sam 5:6–8 RSV)

This passage depicts David as an enemy of the blind and the lame. On his account they are barred access to "the house." But Matthew presents Jesus as the new David, the one with the authority to reverse his ancestor's position. Accordingly, Jesus now welcomes the blind and the lame back into the "house" of the temple and cures them there. Of course, the chief priests and scribes oppose Jesus' messianic overtures. Ironically, they fail to perceive what is evident to even the youngest of children—that Jesus really is the "Son of David." In Matthew's context, therefore, the casting out of the buyers and sellers serves primarily to set the stage for the events that follow. As a result, Matthew's version reveals little about Jesus' objection to temple commerce, but much about Jesus' identity.

As for the cursing of the fig tree, Matthew has disentangled it from the temple incident. It now appears, in its entirety, on the following day:

> When he was going back to the city in the morning, he was hungry. Seeing a fig tree by the road, he went over to it, but found nothing on it except leaves. And he said to it, "May no fruit ever come from you again." And immediately the fig tree withered. When the disciples saw this, they were amazed and said, "How was it that the fig tree withered immediately?" Jesus said to them in reply, "Amen, I say to you, if you have faith and do not waver, not only will you do what has been done to the fig tree, but even if you say to this mountain, 'Be lifted up and thrown into the sea,' it will be done. Whatever you ask for in prayer with faith, you will receive." (Matt 21:18–22 NAB)

For Matthew, the cursing of the fig tree functions as an object lesson for Jesus' disciples about the relationship between faith and miracles. Just as Jesus can immediately cause a full-grown tree to shrivel up, so too can they, with sufficient conviction, perform similar—and even greater—wonders. To what extent (if at all) Matthew still intends to associate the fig tree with the temple is difficult to tell. Certainly the correspondence is not nearly as strong as it is for Mark.

We are left with fairly different conceptions of Jesus' last public actions. The evangelists variously interpret the temple scene as representative of Jesus' curse upon the religious establishment (Mark), his sense of social justice (Luke), his tremendous zeal for his Father's house (John), and his messianic identity (Matthew). The meanings assigned to the withered fig tree are even more polarized. Whereas in Mark's gospel the shriveled plant epitomizes infidelity, in Matthew's it exemplifies faith. Despite these differences, the evangelists' interpretations of these deeds remain entirely consistent with their own understandings of Jesus and his ministry.

It is tempting, of course, to become critical of such subjectivity among the ancient writers. Certainly in our modern society, such preconceived suppositions don't influence our objective judgments! Or do they? Consider a more contemporary public action, such as O. J. Simpson's dramatic, sixty-mile "chase" that transpired on the Los Angeles freeway system on Friday, June 17, 1994. Having been charged in the double murder of his ex-wife, Nicole, and her friend, Ron Goldman, the NFL legend enlisted the aid of his former teammate, Al Cowlings, and evaded police custody for several hours. As Cowlings navigated a white Bronco down the 405 Freeway in Santa Anna, Simpson crouched low in its back seat with a gun to his own head. News helicopters captured the event as ABC, NBC, CBS, CNN, and ESPN all broke into their regularly scheduled programming to broadcast the drama live to an estimated ninety-five million viewers.

Despite the consistency of his deed—after all, everyone saw essentially the same thing—its interpretation differed greatly. Some understood Simpson's flight as an act of pure despair. They reasoned that Simpson had worked a lifetime to establish a successful career and a good reputation. The negative attacks in the press and the pressure of a racially biased investigation had caused Simpson to become depressed and despondent. Simpson's behavior simply underscored his innocence.

Of course, others interpreted Simpson's display as proof of his guilt. They believed Simpson recognized that the evidence mounting against him was irrefutable and that his impending arrest would most likely lead to a lifelong prison sentence—or worse. This left Simpson with no recourse but to become a fugitive from the authorities.

In either case, it seems that one's likely conclusion about Simpson's white Bronco odyssey was determined largely by one's opinion of Simpson prior to this event. Both those who upheld Simpson's innocence and those who suspected his guilt tended to interpret this act compatibly with their previous perspectives.

In this respect the evangelists are no different than we are. Their interpretations of Jesus' actions are premised primarily upon their own notions of who (and what) he is. As we shall see in the next chapter, this principle rings especially true when it comes to the details of Jesus' passion.

Jesus' Passion, Death, and Resurrection

In the first section of this book (chs. 1–3), we considered some of the premises behind Jesus' early years. The second section (chs. 4–7) surveyed underlying contexts that pertain to Jesus' public ministry. In this third and final section (chs. 8–10), we turn to those presuppositions that bear upon what is arguably Jesus' most important legacy: his passion, death, and resurrection. These three topics will occupy the focus of the next three chapters respectively.

8

Jesus' Passion

THE GETHSEMANE SCENE

FOCUS TEXTS: MARK 14:32–52; MATTHEW 26:36–56;
LUKE 22:39–53; JOHN 18:1–12

*A*t the conclusion of chapter 7, we demonstrated how pre conceived notions influence interpretation. We used O. J. Simpson's white Bronco escapade as a modern-day example of this principle in action. If people were asked now, more than a decade later, for their recollections of this particular incident, some common details would probably emerge: the white Bronco, Al Cowlings, the cleared interstate, the news helicopters, the slow-speed "chase," etc.

In addition to these commonalities, there would also be some differences. For instance, those that maintained Simpson's inno cence would probably be more likely to mention the apparent sui cide note Simpson left that day—a note in which he thanked many of his friends and family, begged the press to lay off his kids, sympa thized with the Goldman family, and clung firmly to his innocence. They may also be more likely to recall that throughout his cell-phone calls to the police, Simpson kept insisting that he'd never use the gun he held against them, but only against himself. On the other hand, those that judged Simpson guilty would be more likely to recall that when police eventually took Simpson into custody, he allegedly was in possession of his passport, a large sum of money, his travel bag, and a disguise. Why the differences in detail? It seems our premises not only influence our interpretation of events, they influence our processing and recall of them as well. We are simply more likely to remember those details that conform to our perception of reality.

To illustrate this point another way, suppose a doctor, an auto mechanic, a lawyer, and a physicist simultaneously witness the same car accident. When interviewed by the police, there would no doubt be a certain consistency to their stories. Yet given their backgrounds, we would expect their details to differ. For example, the physicist will likely indicate the forces, speeds, and distances involved in the impact. The doctor will specify injuries to the occupants. The lawyer will identify the cause of the accident and potential liabilities. And the auto mechanic will recount details of damage sustained by the vehicles. Subsequent police reports, newspaper accounts, and insurance claims of the accident will no doubt be influenced by the varying paradigms of the eyewitnesses. Exactly how these documents are influenced depends largely upon what information the investigators receive and which details they deem of greatest importance. These same dynamics are at work in the gospels.

When it comes to Jesus' passion, the records of the evangelists demonstrate substantial agreement. It is in their varying details, however, that we glean insight into the unique paradigms of the authors and their sources. Before turning to these differences, let us first establish those details on which all four agree.

Matthew, Mark, Luke, and John all concur that on the eve before his death, Jesus and his disciples shared a "Last Supper" together. Judas left during that meal to betray Jesus to the Jewish leaders. When Jesus and his disciples had finished eating, they went out to the Mount of Olives (across the Kidron Valley), where they encountered Judas and the authorities. Violence broke out, and one of the disciples severed the ear of the high priest's servant. Jesus was then arrested and taken away for questioning. Meanwhile, Peter followed and, when pressed, denied knowing Jesus three times. At that point, a cock crowed in accordance with Jesus' prediction. The next day, the Jewish authorities brought Jesus to Pilate. Pilate questioned Jesus, but did not find him guilty. He offered to release a prisoner to the Jews, but the crowd chose Barabbas over Jesus. Pilate then consented to Jesus' crucifixion. Jesus was crucified between two others at Golgotha. Lots were cast for his garments, and he was offered something to drink. The inscription designated him as the "King of the Jews." There were a number of women followers who witnessed Jesus' death, including Mary Magdalene. After Jesus expired, Joseph of Arimathea asked Pilate for the body. Pilate approved, so Joseph wrapped Jesus' corpse in linen and laid it in a tomb.

The unanimity described here is fairly impressive. Nevertheless, there are distinctive elements and themes in each of the passion accounts that are often overlooked by modern readers, who tend to combine the stories, as we have discovered with the nativity stories (see ch. 2). Therefore, in order to capture the unique viewpoint of each author and the underlying premises that inform it, we must once again distinguish one version from the other. Because the passion material—from Jesus' Last Supper to his expiration on the cross—is substantially longer than the nativity material (674 verses in four gospels compared to 145 verses in just two gospels), we will confine our analysis to one specific episode: the Gethsemane scene.

Normally, our comparison would proceed chronologically, beginning with Mark. However, Mark's Gethsemane scene presents us with an especially enigmatic character, a young man fleeing naked out of the garden! Who is this individual, and why does he streak through the pages of Mark's gospel? For centuries, this figure has aroused the curiosity of biblical scholars, who have sought earnestly to "reveal" Mark's meaning. Because many factors are involved in the interpretation of this young man, we'll save Mark's version for last. Instead, we'll begin with Matthew's account, since it bears the most similarity to Mark's.

Matthew's Version

And when they had sung a hymn, they went out to the Mount of Olives. . . . Then Jesus went with them to a place called Gethsemane; and he said to his disciples, "Sit here, while I go yonder and pray." And taking with him Peter and the two sons of Zebedee, he began to be sorrowful and troubled. Then he said to them, "My soul is very sorrowful, even to death; remain here, and watch with me." And going a little farther he fell on his face and prayed, "My Father, if it be possible, let this cup pass from me; nevertheless, not as I will, but as thou wilt." (Matt 26:30, 36–39 RSV)

After two thousand years of Christian tradition, it becomes easy to take the location of Jesus' arrest for granted. Gethsemane is situated on the Mount of Olives, a site that has little meaning for most readers today. But for Matthew, the great distress and sorrow experienced by Jesus at this particular spot would have brought another incident to mind.

Second Samuel 15 describes how Absalom, the son of David, sought to seize the throne from his father. Absalom succeeded in swaying the hearts of the Israelites to his cause—including David's trusted counselor, Ahithophel. Forced to flee Jerusalem, David

> went up the ascent of the Mount of Olives, weeping as he went, barefoot and with his head covered; and all the people who were with him covered their heads, and they went up, weeping as they went. And it was told David, "Ahithophel is among the conspirators with Absalom." And David said, "O Lord, I pray thee, turn the counsel of Ahithophel into foolishness." (2 Sam 15:30–31 RSV)

The parallels between Jesus and David are striking. Both ascend the Mount of Olives with their followers. Both experience great sorrow and pray for God's assistance. Both are betrayed by one of their own advisors. Even the plan proposed by Ahithophel appears similar to the one eventually enacted by Judas:

> Let me choose twelve thousand men, and I will set out and pursue David tonight. I will come upon him while he is weary and discouraged, and throw him into a panic; and all the people who are with him will flee. I will strike down the king only. (2 Sam 17:1–2 RSV)

Judas, of course, turns on his master by enlisting the assistance of a fairly large, well-armed force. He, too, strikes at night, when Jesus is weary and discouraged. The disciples are thrown into a panic and flee, and Jesus alone is brought into custody.

Matthew takes the Ahithophel/Judas relationship even further. According to 2 Sam 17:23, when Ahithophel learned that Absalom had decided not to follow his advice, Ahithophel returned home and hung himself. According to Matt 27:5, this is precisely how Judas meets his fate (but cf. Acts 1:18–19, where Judas dies after falling headlong into his own field). That Matthew intended this comparison is suggested by the fact that Ahithophel and Judas are the *only* two biblical personalities to die this way.

Matthew's accentuation of the Davidic history surrounding the Mount of Olives probably comes as little surprise to the reader. We have seen Matthew's presentation of Jesus as the "new David" in his genealogy (ch. 1) and in the temple episode (ch. 7). This motif continues throughout Matthew's Passion Narrative as well. Only in this gospel, for instance, does Jesus ask, at the moment of his arrest:

> Do you think that I cannot appeal to my Father, and he will at once send me more than twelve legions of angels? But how then should the scriptures be fulfilled, that it must be so? (Matt 26:53–54 RSV)

No king, of course, can be captured unless his troops are either defeated or—as Matthew's Jesus intimates—otherwise restrained. Shortly hereafter, the Roman authorities will clothe Jesus in scarlet, crown him with thorns, present him with a reed scepter, kneel before him, and mock him as the "King of the Jews" (Matt 27:27–37). Needless to say, Jesus' investiture is not nearly as pleasant as David's!

While Matthew, and to a lesser extent, Mark, emphasize the correlation between Jesus, David, and the Mount of Olives, neither Luke nor John seems inclined to follow suit.

Luke's Version

> And [Jesus] came out, and went, as was his custom, to the Mount of Olives; and the disciples followed him. And when he came to the place he said to them, "Pray that you may not enter into temptation." And he withdrew from them about a stone's throw, and knelt down and prayed, "Father if thou art willing, remove this cup from me; nevertheless not my will, but thine, be done." . . . And when he rose from prayer, he came to the disciples and found them sleeping for sorrow, and he said to them, "Why do you sleep? Rise and pray that you may not enter into temptation." (Luke 22:39–42, 45–46 RSV)

Compared to Matthew and Mark, Jesus' tremendous grief is noticeably absent here. Only the disciples are sorrowful. Presumably, the relative ease with which Luke's Jesus handles his approaching fate prompted some ancient scribe to add vv. 43–44, which are missing from our earliest and most reliable manuscripts:

> [And to strengthen him an angel from heaven appeared to him. He was in such agony and he prayed so fervently that his sweat became like drops of blood falling on the ground.] (NAB)

It is somewhat ironic that the popular conception of Jesus' "agony" in the garden is ultimately derived from verses that, although ancient, were most likely not original to this gospel.

Luke not only downplays Jesus' inner turmoil, he also presents a different dynamic between Jesus and his disciples. According to Matthew and Mark, Jesus implores Peter, James, and John to "remain and watch with me." When Jesus returns and finds them sleeping, he asks Peter, "Could you not watch with me one hour?" Three times Jesus enjoins them to stay awake and pray. Three times he returns to find them asleep. The inability of the disciples to keep vigil with Jesus, even for just a little while, certainly adds to the heartache of the scene. But in Luke's account, Jesus merely asks the disciples to pray that they may not enter into temptation. He returns only once and finds that their grief has exhausted them. Given this link between sorrow and slumber, it is possible to take Jesus' question, "Why do you sleep?" less as an objection to their behavior, and more as an encouragement not to worry. Thus, in Matthew and Mark's version, Jesus appears to seek support from his disciples; in Luke's version, Jesus offers it to them.

Jesus' compassionate outreach continues throughout the remainder of Luke's gospel. For instance, when the servant's ear is severed during the scuffle in Gethsemane, only Luke relates that Jesus restored it (22:51). As he endures his crucifixion, Luke's Jesus is the only one to exclaim, "Father, forgive them, they know not what they do!" (23:34 NAB). And only in Luke's gospel does Jesus, on the verge of death, welcome the repentant thief into paradise with him (23:43). Collectively, these elements disclose Luke's tendency to perceive Jesus as an empathetic and compassionate Messiah.

John's Version

If *compassionate* best describes Luke's Jesus, then *resolute* characterizes John's. When John's Jesus arrives at the garden, there is no "agony" scene. Rather, Jesus' entourage immediately encounters Judas and the authorities (John 18:2–3). Thus, the disciples never sleep, and Jesus offers no prayer concerning the conflict between his will and God's. In fact, when Peter attempts to prevent the arrest, Jesus asks him, "Shall I not drink the cup which the Father has given me?" (18:11 RSV).

When the mob arrives, Jesus continues to demonstrate his determination to carry out his Father's will:

Knowing all that was to befall him, [Jesus] came forward and said to them, "Whom do you seek?" They answered him, "Jesus of Nazareth." Jesus said to them, "I am he." . . . When he said to them, "I am he," they drew back and fell to the ground. Again he asked them, "Whom do you seek?" And they said, "Jesus of Nazareth." Jesus answered, "I told you that I am he; so, if you seek me, let these men go." (18:4–8 RSV)

John records no "signal" by Judas as the other evangelists do. Instead, Jesus himself confronts the crowd, which draws back and seems reluctant to seize him. Jesus practically has to tell them what to do!

Indeed, John's Jesus is so intent on proceeding with his death, at times he almost appears to orchestrate it. As an example, consider Matthew and Mark's version of the Last Supper, where Judas dips his bread into the bowl with Jesus and then departs inconspicuously (Mark 14:20//Matt 26:23). By contrast, John's Jesus dips the morsel himself, hands it to Judas, and commands him, "What you are going to do, do quickly!" (John 13:26–27 NAB). Likewise, according to the Synoptic Gospels, Simon of Cyrene is recruited to carry Jesus' cross (Mark 15:21//Matt 27:32//Luke 23:26). But John's Jesus carries it himself (John 19:17). In each case, John conceives of Jesus as playing an active part in his fate. Even Jesus' final words, "It is accomplished!" convey a sense of achievement at having successfully fulfilled his purpose.

Having surveyed three of the Gethsemane scenes, we can now briefly summarize our findings. Matthew incorporates elements that serve to identify Jesus as the Davidic Messiah. Luke presents Jesus as the compassionate one who continues to reach out to others, even in the midst of his own suffering. John depicts Jesus as completely determined to undergo his death in accordance with his Father's will. These varying premises help to explain the differing—even conflicting—details in Gethsemane and elsewhere in Jesus' passion.

Mark's Version

What about Mark? As indicated above, Mark's Gethsemane scene corresponds closely to Matthew's. The most blatant difference occurs during Jesus' arrest:

And immediately, while [Jesus] was still speaking, Judas came, one of the twelve, and with him a crowd with swords and clubs, from the chief priests and the scribes and the elders. . . . And they laid hands on him and seized him. . . . And [the disciples] all forsook him and fled. And a young man followed him, with nothing but a linen cloth about his body; and they seized him, but he left the linen cloth and ran away naked. (Mark 14:43, 46, 50–52 RSV)

None of the other evangelists mention the young man who flees naked from Gethsemane. Who is he, and why has Mark written of him? The explanations offered down through the ages are myriad. They range from the mundane—he was a local resident drawn to the garden by his curiosity—to the outrageous—he was Jesus' homosexual lover, whose secret rendezvous was suddenly interrupted. It seems Mark's virtual silence about this individual has provided fertile ground for speculation.

Traditionally, two questions have driven the interpretation of this scene. First, is Mark thinking here of a specific, historical person, or is the significance of this young man primarily symbolic? Second, to what extent did Mark seek to associate the naked young man with the young man who later appears to the women at the tomb? Mark describes this second young man at the conclusion of his gospel:

And entering the tomb [the women] saw a young man sitting on the right side, dressed in a white robe; and they were amazed. And he said to them, "Do not be amazed; you seek Jesus of Nazareth, who was crucified. He has risen, he is not here; see the place where they laid him. But go, tell his disciples and Peter that he is going before you to Galilee; there you will see him, as he told you." And they went out and fled from the tomb; for trembling and astonishment had come upon them; and they said nothing to any one, for they were afraid. (Mark 16:5–8 RSV)

The varying answers to the above questions pose several possibilities for the naked young man.

THE NAKED YOUNG MAN AS A HISTORICAL FIGURE

Some scholars have proposed that the young man who flees from the garden and the young man dressed in white are literally the same person. These are, after all, the only two places where Mark employs the term, *young man*. Furthermore, at no point does Mark designate the latter as an *angel* even though all the other evangelists do.

If these two young men are in fact one, the implications are profound. This nameless follower would be the first witness to the resurrection instead of Mary (in Matthew and John) or the disciples (in Luke). Moreover, according to Mark, he is the only *faithful* witness. In 16:8, the apparent ending to this gospel, the women flee—much like the disciples during Jesus' arrest—and fail to spread the report entrusted to them. Mark's account, therefore, could be seen as bolstering the reputation of this young man over and against that of Jesus' disciples.

So who was he? Because of his relative anonymity, there is the suspicion that he was someone familiar to Mark's community. Details about him may not have been divulged simply because they were presumed to be known. Accordingly, many take this young man to be none other than Mark himself. Perhaps Mark's authority was at odds with that of the disciples, the more established pillars of the early church. This theory could account for Mark's relatively negative portrayal of the Twelve. It could also explain why additional gospels—those more favorable to Jesus' inner circle—emerged in the wake of Mark's.

Although this theory has much to commend it, its chief difficulty is the lack of detail about the young man between Gethsemane and the tomb. One would expect Mark, or another such contender, to capitalize on the intervening period by explaining his radical transformation from naked deserter to clothed proclaimer. Such strategy would afford him a golden opportunity to solidify his authority in the early church. But this doesn't happen.

Furthermore, there are good reasons to believe that Mark envisioned the young man at the tomb not as a human being, but as an angel. Among the most compelling ones are the initial words of comfort and the reaction of the women. The phrase, "Do not be amazed," is a standard reassurance pronounced by heavenly messengers, as we have seen in Gabriel's appearance to Zechariah (Luke 1:13) and Mary (1:30); for other examples, see Judg 6:23; Dan 10:12, 19; Tob 12:17; Luke 2:10; Acts 27:24; Rev 1:17. In much the same way, fear and trembling are typical responses for the subjects of these spiritual encounters (so Dan 10:7–11, 15–18; Tob 12:16; Luke 1:12, 29; 2:9). In fact, while Mark's designation of the angel as a "young man" is curious, it is not entirely unprecedented. This label is applied to the otherworldly beings who guard the temple treasury in 2 Macc 3:26, and to the angel Raphael before he is recognized as such in Tobit 5–12.

Assuming Mark's second young man is an angel, who is the first? It still remains possible, of course, that the naked young man is Mark. Perhaps he has chosen to record this incident precisely because it draws upon his own personal experience. According to Acts 12:12, Mark's mother owned a house in Jerusalem where the first Christians used to gather together. Some have speculated that this is the same house where Jesus celebrated his Last Supper. If so, then perhaps Mark roused himself from bed, lightly clad, and followed Jesus' party to Gethsemane.

While theoretically possible, this scenario falters again on Mark's reticence to identify himself. As is evident from the examples of Matthew and John (especially), any contact between Jesus and the named evangelist was usually accorded special prominence. This practice lent credibility and distinction to the gospel. If Mark was present at Gethsemane or even more so, if his house was the site of Jesus' final meal, we should expect him not only to acknowledge this fact, but to call it to attention.

If, then, the naked young man is not Mark, his historical identity can only be a matter of conjecture. Perhaps Mark meant to embarrass this individual. But if this were the case, why not name him? Whether the event happened or not—and there is little reason to assume it didn't—it seems likely that Mark recorded it with another, more symbolic purpose in mind.

THE NAKED YOUNG MAN AS A SYMBOLIC FIGURE

Even though Mark probably considers the second young man to be an angel, it is still possible that he employs the term "young man" because he intends a comparison between these two figures. The first young man is stripped naked at the moment of Jesus' arrest. The second young man, clothed in white, delivers the first announcement of Jesus' resurrection. If the contrast is indeed deliberate, what does it mean?

The roots of the symbolism must lie in the disparity between nakedness and white clothing. We can appeal to certain premises to help us decipher these symbols. In the Jewish Wisdom literature, nakedness is occasionally associated with death:

Naked I came forth from my mother's womb, and naked shall I go back again. (Job 1:21 NAB)

As he came forth from his mother's womb, so again shall he depart, naked as he came. (Eccl 5:14 NAB)

Corresponding to this imagery, white robes are given to the faithful believers who have been raised to new life in the book of Revelation:

He who conquers shall be clad thus in white garments, and I will not blot his name out of the book of life; I will confess his name before my Father and before his angels. (Rev 3:5 RSV)

I saw . . . the souls of those who had been slain for the word of God and for the witness they had borne. . . . They were each given a white robe and told to rest a little longer. (Rev 6:9, 11 RSV)

Against this background, some have proposed that Mark's two young men may serve to underscore the narrative movement of Jesus' passion, from the official beginning of Jesus' death to the proclamation of his new life.

Unfortunately, while this symbolism makes good sense and fits the context of the Passion Narrative, Mark himself does not appear to subscribe to it. If Mark did foreshadow Jesus' death with nakedness, then he has missed out on the perfect chance to solidify this connection later on in his gospel. According to Mark, Jesus is ridiculed by the Roman soldiers immediately following sentencing (Mark 15:16–20). They dress him in royal garb and pretend to pay him homage. Then,

when they had mocked him, they stripped him of the purple cloak, *dressed him in his own clothes,* and led him out to crucify him. (15:20 NAB, emphasis added)

Although Jesus is now being led off to death, Mark specifies that the Roman guards slipped him back into his own clothes. This, despite the fact that they had to immediately disrobe him again—an action Mark *fails* to mention—in order to divide up his garments (15:24)! It seems incredible that Mark would neglect this opportunity to exemplify his meaning if he truly associated nakedness with Jesus' death.

In fact, if the OT is an accurate gauge, death is not the first thing that the naked young man would have conveyed to Mark's original audience. Nakedness is mentioned some thirty-eight times in the Hebrew Scriptures. In the vast majority of instances, it is directly connected with shame: the shame of sin (Genesis 3), drunkenness (Gen 9:20–28; Hab 2:15), defeat or punishment (Deut 28:48; 2 Chr 28:15; Hos 2:3; Amos 2:16; Ezek 16:39; 23:10), poverty (Job 22:6; 24:7, 10; Isa 58:7; Ezek 18:7, 16), and sexual immorality (Isa 57:8; Ezek 16:36–37; 23:18, 29). Mark's earliest readers, therefore, would have correlated the young man's nakedness primarily with shame.

What of the white raiment? This image frequently denotes supernatural glory, a meaning that even Mark ascribes to it:

> As I watched, thrones were set up and the Ancient One took his throne. His clothing was snow bright, and the hair on his head as white as wool. (Dan 7:9 NAB)

> And [Jesus] was transfigured before them, and his clothes became dazzling white, such as no fuller on earth could bleach them. (Mark 9:2–3 NAB)

Given these premises, then, it is much more likely that Mark conceived of the two young men as representing shame and glory. The glory, of course, is obvious. Jesus has triumphed over the tomb. But in what manner is the Gethsemane scene shameful?

It is tempting to assume that Mark associates shame with the general disgrace of incarceration. In this way, Mark's two young men could be read in a progressive sense, from the ignominy of Jesus' detainment to his victory over death.

There are, however, two difficulties with this interpretation. First, in the ancient world, captives—especially prisoners of war— were often stripped naked as a sign of their defeat. Thus, we should expect Jesus, the one captured, not his follower, the escapee, to be exposed. Another objection is found in 16:8, where the women *flee* (the same verb used of the naked young man) from the tomb. If this verse is truly the conclusion of Mark's gospel—as our earliest and most reliable manuscripts indicate—then it represents a slight regression in the plot. In other words, as it now stands, Mark's narrative advances from shame (naked young man fleeing Gethsemane) to glory (clothed young man at the tomb) and then back again toward shame (women fleeing the tomb).

Given the immediate context, Mark evidently has another, more specific meaning in mind. Just prior to entering the garden, Jesus predicted Peter's denial in the presence of the disciples. Peter, however,

> vehemently replied, "Even though I should have to die with you, I will not deny you." *And they all spoke similarly.* (14:31 NAB, emphasis added)

Shortly thereafter, those very same men who had earnestly pledged their lives to Jesus flee in the face of his enemies. Given this turn of events, Mark almost certainly understands the shame not as applying to the humiliation of Jesus' arrest *per se,* but as epitomizing the action of Jesus' "loyalists." This would explain why Mark neglects to identify the young man beyond "a certain follower of Jesus." Mark's generic designation lends itself well to collective comparison. Just as this anonymous character is stripped of his clothes and runs off naked, so are the disciples stripped of their courage and dignity as they abandon their master in his hour of need. Mark's specification that the lad was lightly clothed to begin with may further insinuate something about the mettle of Jesus' disciples from the start. (Although Mark never vindicates the disciples, the later evangelists are careful to "set the record straight.")

This interpretation also lends perspective to Mark's conclusion. Sandwiched as it is between the flight of the disciples and the flight of the women, the supernatural glory of Jesus' resurrection, signified by the young man clothed in white, now stands in sharp contrast to the shameful failure of Jesus' followers. In the midst of their shortcomings, Jesus emerges triumphant.

With our survey of the Gethsemane scene complete, we can now review the distinct perspectives of each of the gospels. Like the follow-up reports of the car accident, the accounts of Jesus' passion vary according to the information that the evangelists received and the weight that they assigned to certain details. Matthew's elements underscore Jesus' Davidic kingship, Luke's emphasize Jesus' compassion, and John's portray Jesus' determination to accomplish his God-given purpose. Mark, on the other hand, uses the figure of the naked young man to highlight the shame of Jesus' disciples. Having pledged their undying loyalty to him, they desert Jesus just when he needs them most. Of course, this is not the end of Mark's story. At the conclusion of his gospel, the young man reemerges—this time clothed in white—to signal the eminence of Jesus' resurrection. Despite the failure of his followers, Jesus himself is gloriously vindicated.

9

Jesus' Death

As we move now from Jesus' passion to his death, we will leave behind our cross-sectional approach to the gospels and concentrate more narrowly on just one of them: John's account. At the beginning of chapter 8, we noted the passion details on which all four of the evangelists agree. Not included in that list—because of John—is the nature and date of Jesus' farewell gathering with his disciples.

According to the Synoptics, Jesus' Last Supper coincided with the Jewish feast of Passover, the beginning of the week-long Festival of Unleavened Bread:

> And on the first day of Unleavened Bread, when they sacrificed the passover lamb, his disciples said to him, "Where will you have us go and prepare for you to eat the passover?" (Mark 14:12 RSV)

> Now on the first day of Unleavened Bread the disciples came to Jesus, saying, "Where will you have us prepare for you to eat the passover?" (Matt 26:17 RSV)

> Then came the day of Unleavened Bread, on which the passover lamb had to be sacrificed. So Jesus sent Peter and John, saying, "Go and prepare the passover for us, that we may eat it." (Luke 22:7–8 RSV)

The Torah establishes the evening between the fourteenth and fifteenth of Nisan, a month that overlaps March and April, as the official start of Passover (Exod 12:6; Lev 23:5–6; Num 28:16–17).

This reckoning, which can be confusing to those unaccustomed to it, is based on the lunar calendar. Accordingly, the days begin at sunset of the previous "day" and last until the following sunset. Assuming Jesus' disciples approached him *before* evening, as the narratives suggest, the above exchange must have transpired on the fourteenth of Nisan. This would have been on Thursday morning or afternoon, on the so-called day of preparation. Although Matthew and Mark refer to this as the "first" day of Unleavened Bread, this designation was typically reserved for the fifteenth of Nisan, the day that the Passover meal was actually consumed (i.e., Thursday evening). This explains why Luke omits the reference. According to the Synoptics, then, Passover would have fallen between Thursday and Friday evenings.

The Synoptics concur that Jesus was arrested and tried by the Jewish authorities on Thursday night. On Friday, Jesus was taken before Pilate, sentenced, and crucified. Following his death, Jesus was hastily buried just before sundown in order to avoid violating the Sabbath, since the Jewish law prohibited most work from being done on this day. The women then returned to the tomb on "the first day of the week" (Sunday) to complete Jesus' burial. It was on this, the "third" day of Jesus' death, that he was raised to life.

John's timetable parallels much of this. According to John, Jesus ate his Last Supper, was arrested, and was questioned by the Jewish authorities on Thursday evening. He appeared before Pilate, and was sentenced, crucified, died, and buried on Friday. He then rose from the dead on Sunday. The only chronological discrepancy is the day on which John's Passover falls.

John notes that Jesus arrived in Bethany six days before Passover (John 12:1). However, he neglects to indicate the number of days that elapse between this arrival and the Last Supper. According to 13:1, Jesus and his disciples simply share a meal "before the feast of Passover" (RSV). That John's Passover is not on Thursday, as it is in the Synoptics, is clear. So when is it? John reveals this information to his readers only gradually. Later, John writes that the Jewish authorities

> led Jesus from the house of Caiaphas to the praetorium. It was early. They themselves did not enter the praetorium, so that they might not be defiled, but might eat the passover. (18:28 RSV)

By Friday morning, the Passover had not yet occurred. Obviously it is nearing, but its exact date remains unknown to John's readers. In fact, it is not until Jesus' condemnation later on that day that John offers a definitive answer regarding its timing:

> [Pilate] brought Jesus out and sat down on the judgment seat at a place called The Pavement, and in Hebrew, Gabbatha. Now it was the day of Preparation of the Passover; it was about the sixth hour. He said to the Jews, "Behold your King!" They cried out, "Away with him, away with him, crucify him!" Pilate said to them, "Shall I crucify your King?" The chief priests answered, "We have no king but Caesar." Then he handed him over to them to be crucified." (19:13–16 RSV)

Because John records this moment as taking place on "the day of Preparation of the Passover," Passover itself must have fallen on Saturday. Indeed, this assessment is confirmed immediately after Jesus' death:

> Since it was the day of Preparation, in order to prevent the bodies from remaining on the cross on the sabbath, *(for that sabbath was a high day)*, the Jews asked Pilate that their legs might be broken, and that they might be taken away. (19:31 RSV, emphasis added)

We are left, then, with three witnesses (Matthew, Mark, and Luke) who claim that Jesus and his disciples celebrated Passover, and only one (John) who maintains that Passover occurred later, after Jesus had died. If we assign greater weight to the testimony of the Synoptics, then we must presume that John *moved* Passover. But why would he deliberately change the date of this feast?

The key to understanding John's calendar lies with the notion that the timing of a given event sometimes helps to convey its meaning. A good example of this principle involves a couple of religious holidays. The Christian church celebrates the feast day of John the Baptist on June 24. According to legend, this was the day of his birth, but of course, the precise date would have been nearly impossible to verify. Why, then, June 24? This date coincides with the summer solstice, the period at which the sun's trajectory is at its zenith, marking the longest day of the year. From this point forward, the arcs of the sun's path over the horizon gradually diminish and the days shorten. But why make the connection between John the Baptist and the summer solstice? Consider John's words about Jesus:

Passion Timetables Compared

SYNOPTICS (LUNAR DAY)	SOLAR DAYS	JOHN (LUNAR DAY)
14 Nisan *Day of Preparation* lambs slaughtered	Thursday morning and afternoon	**13 Nisan**
15 Nisan *Passover* Last Supper Gethsemane arrest Jewish trial	Thursday evening	**14 Nisan** *Day of Preparation* Last Supper Gethsemane arrest Jewish trial
taken before Pilate sentenced crucified buried	Friday morning and afternoon	taken before Pilate sentenced crucified buried
16 Nisan Sabbath (work forbidden)	Friday evening to Saturday evening	**15 Nisan** *Passover* Sabbath (work forbidden)
17 Nisan resurrection	Saturday evening to Sunday evening	**16 Nisan** resurrection

"He must increase; I must decrease" (John 3:30 NAB). From John's feast day forward, the days decrease.

As for Jesus, the Christian church celebrates his birthday on December 25. Again, this date would have been difficult to verify. (In fact, taking cues from Luke's gospel, most scholars think he was actually born in the spring.) So, why December 25? Here, too, the timing conveys a certain meaning. December 25 coincides with the winter solstice, the shortest day of the year. From this point forward, the sun's descending trajectory is reversed, and the days grow longer. In the ancient world, this event marked the annual Feast of the Unconquerable Sun—the date on which the powers of light began to beat back the forces of darkness. Since Christians take Jesus to be the Light of the World, their adaptation of this date was only natural. Thus, December 25 became known as the "Feast of the Unconquerable Son."

In both these instances, the dates of the feast days lend meaning to their interpretation. The same is true of John's timetable. His placement of Passover on the day after Jesus' death makes perfect sense in light of certain premises about this Jewish holiday.

Passover celebrates the liberation of God's chosen people from their slavery in Egypt. Specifically, it commemorates the Hebrews' last night, when God struck down all the first-born Egyptians. The book of Exodus recounts the instructions for survival that God provided to Moses. In turn, Moses communicated these instructions to the people.

Moses ordered the head of each Hebrew family to obtain a lamb for their household. The lamb needed to be "a year old male, without blemish" and must be kept until the fourteenth day of Nisan, when the whole assembly of Israel would kill their lambs in between the two evenings (Exod 12:5–6). The Hebrews were then enjoined to take a bunch of hyssop and dip it in the lamb's blood which is in the basin, and touch the lintel and the two doorposts of their homes with the blood. This was done so that when the Lord came through to slay the Egyptians, he could "pass over" those doors marked with blood and thus spare the Hebrews (Exod 12:22–23).

As for the rest of the lamb, it was to be roasted whole. Its meat was not to be taken outside the house, nor were any of its bones to be broken (Exod 12:46). It was to be eaten with unleavened bread and bitter herbs (Exod 12:8). The unleavened bread, which would be consumed for the next seven days, signified the haste of the slaves' departure. Presumably, there was no time to spare waiting for their yeast to rise. The bitter herbs signified the bitterness of their captivity.

All of the evangelists agree that Jesus and his disciples had traveled up to Jerusalem in connection with Passover. According to Josephus, the number of individuals that made this annual pilgrimage was considerable. For instance, in the year that Jerusalem was besieged (ca. 70 CE), Josephus estimates that some 256,500 lambs were slaughtered for Passover. Figuring one lamb for every ten people, Josephus sets the number of pilgrims in Jerusalem that year at 2,565,000 (*J.W.* 6.9.3).

Obviously such an immense crowd poses certain logistical challenges. For instance, how does one go about slaughtering 256,500
lambs within the designated time frame ("between the two evenings")? The conservative interpreters of this phrase took it to designate the period between sunset and actual darkness. Of course, such
a brief window would make this massive task impossible. Thus, the
Mishnah offers a more liberal interpretation. It considers any lamb
that is sacrificed between midday (when the sun begins to descend)
and evening legitimate (*m. Pesah.* 5.3).

In light of these premises, John's portrayal of Jesus' condemnation "at the sixth hour" (noon) on the day of preparation can hardly
be accidental. Jesus' death sentence comes at the very same time that
the Passover lambs would have begun to be slaughtered. That John is
fully aware of the significance of this "hour" is evidenced by his anticipation of it throughout this gospel:

> So they sought to arrest [Jesus]; but no one laid hands on him, because
> his hour had not yet come. (John 7:30 RSV)

> These words [Jesus] spoke in the treasury, as he taught in the temple;
> but no one arrested him, because his hour had not yet come. (8:20
> RSV)

> "Now is my soul troubled. And what shall I say? 'Father, save me from
> this hour'? No, for this purpose I have come to this hour." (12:27 RSV)

> Now before the feast of the Passover, when Jesus knew that his hour
> had come to depart out of this world to the Father . . . (13:1 RSV)

John's Passover chronology, therefore, serves to connect Jesus'
slaying with the slaying of the lambs. But this is not the only detail
that facilitates their comparison. Consider the initial words out of
the mouth of John the Baptist when he sees Jesus approaching him
for the very first time: "Behold, the Lamb of God, who takes away
the sin of the world!" (1:29 RSV). The Baptist repeats these words the
following day: "Behold, the Lamb of God!" (1:36 RSV). John's is the
only gospel to apply this title to Jesus.

At least two other peculiarities enable John to present Jesus as
the "Lamb of God." From his cross, John's Jesus expresses his thirst.
In response, the Roman guards "put a sponge full of the vinegar
on hyssop and held it to his mouth" (19:29 RSV). According to the

other evangelists, the instrument used to elevate the vinegar-soaked sponge is a "reed" (Mark 15:36//Matt 27:48). A reed would have been eminently more suitable for this task. As 1 Kgs 4:33 suggests ("[Solomon] spoke of trees, from the cedar that is in Lebanon to the hyssop that grows out of the wall" [RSV]) hyssop is one of the humblest of plants. It is a leafy shrub, usually associated with Syrian marjoram. Its absorbency and flexibility make it a fine candidate for sprinkling liquids (see Lev 14:4–7, 49–52; Num 19:6, 18; Heb 9:19), but rather impractical for raising aloft a saturated sponge. So why does John write of it here? Given the context, John's reference evokes Passover, and the hyssop that was used to apply the blood of the lamb to the doorposts and lintels of the Hebrews' homes. The hyssop, therefore, enables John to underscore the relationship between Jesus and the sacrificial lambs.

John solidifies his portrayal of Jesus as the Lamb of God with one last detail. According to John, after Jesus died

> the Jews asked Pilate that [the legs of those crucified] might be broken, and they might be taken away. So the soldiers came and broke the legs of the first, and of the other who had been crucified with him; but when they came to Jesus and saw that he was already dead, they did not break his legs. (John 19:31–33 RSV)

Again, John's gospel is the only one to record this scene. The Jews, anxious to get the bodies out of the way before Passover, request that the legs be broken. (A victim of crucifixion would use his legs to push himself up in order to alleviate the pressure on his chest from the weight of his body as he hung on his cross. This act, painful as it was, enabled him to breathe. Breaking the legs incapacitates them and so forces them to succumb to asphyxiation.) Although the guards break the legs of those around him, Jesus is already dead. His legs, therefore, are spared. John sees in this incident a fulfillment of Scripture. As noted above, the Passover regulations required that none of the bones of the sacrificial lamb could be broken. That Jesus also remains "unbroken" after his death confirms his status as an acceptable sacrifice.

John thus presents Jesus as the new Lamb of God by accentuating the timing of Jesus' death, the title bestowed upon him, the reference to hyssop, and the unbroken legs. One question now remains. Why does John go to such lengths to affiliate Jesus with the Passover lamb?

The Passover lamb offered the most suitable paradigm by which John could understand and explain Jesus' atonement. The Jewish members of John's audience would have known the crucial role paschal lambs played in Israel's liberation. The death of these animals spared the Hebrews from the fate of the Egyptians, and consequently led to their release from slavery. In much the same way, John perceives Jesus' death as undertaken on behalf of others. Jesus dies for all those enslaved to sin, so that they might not suffer the condemnation of sinners, but might enjoy the freedom of eternal life. This theology permeates John's gospel:

> For God so loved the world that he gave his only Son, so that everyone who believes in him might not perish but might have eternal life. For God did not send his Son into the world to condemn the world, but that the world might be saved through him. (John 3:16–17 NAB)

> Whoever hears my word and believes in the one who sent me has eternal life and will not come to condemnation, but has passed from death to life. (5:24 NAB)

> [The Jews] answered him, "We are descendants of Abraham and have never been enslaved to anyone. How can you say, 'You will become free'?" Jesus answered them, "Amen, amen, I say to you, everyone who commits sin is a slave of sin. A slave does not remain in a household forever, but a son always remains. So if a son frees you, then you will truly be free. (8:31–36 NAB)

John's portrayal of Jesus as the Lamb of God is thus premised upon the Passover sacrifice. Just as the lambs' blood once saved the Hebrews, so now Jesus' blood saves those who believe in him.

Before concluding this chapter, there is one final point to be made regarding John's timetable. Earlier, we assumed that since three of the evangelists were in agreement, John must have been responsible for repositioning Passover. John's theological agenda further raises the suspicion that his chronological sequence is contrived. Nevertheless, there are a number of good reasons to judge John's time frame as actually being more historically accurate than that of the Synoptics.

First off, the astronomical data indicates that the fourteenth of Nisan fell on a Friday (as John claims) in 30 and 33 CE. However, there is no point between 27 and 34 CE when the fifteenth of Nisan would have fallen on a Friday (as the Synoptics propose).

Second, there is the matter of Jewish law. Because of the solar calendar, most Christians assume that Jesus died the day *after* his Last Supper. But according to Jewish (lunar) reckoning, these events occurred on the *same* day. If the Synoptic accounts are correct, then Jesus' arrest, trial, sentencing, crucifixion, and burial all took place on the fifteenth of Nisan, the first day of the Feast of Passover. This much activity is difficult to justify in light of the Torah's repeated injunctions forbidding it:

> The fifteenth day of this month is the LORD's feast of Unleavened Bread. For seven days you shall eat unleavened bread. On the first of these days you shall hold a sacred assembly and do no sort of work. (Lev 23:6–7 NAB)

> This day shall be a memorial feast for you, which all your generations shall celebrate with pilgrimage to the LORD, as a perpetual institution. For seven days you must eat unleavened bread. . . . On the first day you shall hold a sacred assembly, and likewise on the seventh. On these days you shall not do any sort of work, except to prepare the food that everyone needs. (Exod 12:14–16 NAB)

> On the fourteenth day of the first month falls the Passover of the LORD, and the fifteenth day of this month is the pilgrimage feast. For seven days unleavened bread is to be eaten. On the first of these days you shall hold a sacred assembly, and do no sort of work. (Num 28:16–18 NAB)

Given these stipulations, it is highly unlikely that the Sanhedrin in general—and Joseph of Arimathea in particular—would have been so industrious on such a venerable day.

A third objection to the Synoptic schedule comes, ironically enough, from the gospel narratives themselves. According to Matthew and Mark, the chief priests and scribes sought to arrest Jesus and kill him just two days before the Passover. They specifically plan *not* to seize Jesus "during the feast, lest there be a tumult of the people" (Mark 14:1–2 RSV//Matt 26:1–5). Of course, the Synoptic timetable blatantly contradicts this strategy—they arrest and kill Jesus right in the middle of Passover! Given the length of the festival and the opportunity at hand, it would have made more sense for them to dispose of Jesus ahead of time, especially if they feared he'd rally the masses against them.

All of this evidence suggests that the Synoptic authors probably coincided Jesus' death with Passover in order to link these two events together theologically (as John does). Does this mean these evangelists deliberately falsified their information? Not necessarily. It appears to have been common knowledge that Jesus died *around* the time of Passover. More than a decade before the first gospel was written, for example, Paul had already referred to Jesus as the paschal lamb (1 Cor 5:7). However, uncertainty about the *precise* date of Jesus' death may have led the Synoptic evangelists to assign it to Passover in keeping with this tradition.

Regardless of where Passover really fell that year, all four of the evangelists evidently agree that the *meaning* of Jesus' death is signified, in part, by its *timing*. John spells this out most explicitly. The Lamb of God has been sacrificed. On his account, freedom is now at hand.

10

Jesus' Resurrection

CONSIDERING THE ALTERNATIVES

FOCUS TEXTS: MARK 16:1–8; MATTHEW 28:11–20;
LUKE 24:1–53; JOHN 20:1–21:25

*W*hen it comes down to it, Jesus' claim to be the Son of God rests neither with his genealogy nor with his birth, neither with his baptism nor with his miracles and teachings, neither with his passion nor even with his death. Jesus' claim to be the Son of God stands or falls principally upon his resurrection from the dead. This event forms the linchpin of Christian doctrine, and the foundation of Christianity itself. Its significance cannot be overstated.

Consider Josephus's observations about the variety of false prophets and messianic pretenders circulating throughout Palestine during the first century (e.g., *J. W.* 2.258–263; 6.285–288; *Ant.* 20.167–172). They too gathered disciples, preached the coming of God's reign, performed miraculous signs and wonders, and were persecuted by the Roman authorities. Today, most of them remain completely unknown to us. By comparison, few individuals have had a greater impact on Western civilization than Jesus. What is the difference between them and him? The difference is the resurrection.

It is not the restoration to life that is so unique. The gospels maintain that Jesus raised at least three individuals, including Lazarus, the widow's son, and Jairus's daughter. Furthermore, the Bible includes stories of Elijah reviving a Shunammite child (2 Kgs 4:8–37), Peter raising Tabitha (Acts 9:36–42), and Paul resuscitating Eutychus (Acts 20:7–12). Rather, it is Jesus' previous assertion that he would rise from the dead that, in conjunction with the purported fulfillment of this act, is so amazing.

For the record, not even Harry Houdini, the greatest escape artist ever known, could pull off a stunt like this. But he tried! Prior to his untimely death on October 31, 1926, Harry and his wife, Bess, collaborated upon a secret code they intended to use to contact each other "from the other side." For years following Harry's death, Bess consulted with mediums and spiritists who all claimed they had reached Harry. However, the code was never cracked. On Halloween night, 1936—precisely one decade after Harry's death—Bess participated in a nationally broadcasted séance at the Knickerbocker Hotel in Hollywood. This, too, proved a disappointment. At the end of the program, Bess announced:

> Houdini did not come through. My last hope is gone. I do not believe that Houdini can come back to me, or to anyone else. . . . The Houdini Shrine has burned for ten years. I now, reverently . . . turn out the light. It is finished. Good night, Harry![1]

The Great Houdini was evidently incapable of returning from the dead. Yet all of the gospels claim that Jesus succeeded. Their accounts of his resurrection, however, vary considerably.

Mark provides the least amount of information. In fact, if we presume Mark's ending at 16:8, the risen Jesus never does make an appearance. Rather, Mark simply affirms Jesus' resurrection through the words of the young man at the tomb: "Do not be amazed; you seek Jesus of Nazareth, who was crucified. He has risen, he is not here" (16:6 RSV). According to Matthew, Jesus manifests himself twice. He first greets the women as they make their way back from the tomb (Matt 28:8–10), and then he meets with the eleven on a mountain in Galilee (28:16–20). Luke records three appearances. Jesus approaches two of his followers on the road to Emmaus (Luke 24:13–32), contacts Peter (24:34), and then reveals himself to his disciples in Jerusalem (24:36–49). John describes more appearances by the risen Jesus than any other evangelist. On Sunday, Jesus presents himself first to Mary Magdalene at the tomb (John 20:11–18) and then to the disciples gathered together in a closed room (20:19–23). Eight days later, Jesus returns again to the same house, this time, specifically to Thomas (20:26–29). After that, seven of the disciples encounter Jesus while they are out fishing (21:1–14).

Given the inherent improbability of this act and the obvious discrepancies among the witnesses, it is only natural to become skeptical of it. To some, of course, the questioning of Jesus' resurrection may seem sacrilegious. But evidence from the gospels indicates that the evangelists themselves expected and even presupposed the objections of their readers. Because such objections are specifically anticipated by these accounts, we can consider them in light of more "reasonable" explanations.

Wrong or Empty Tomb

All four of the gospels agree that it was Joseph of Arimathea who laid Jesus' body in a nearby tomb. Some propose that he accidentally laid it in the wrong tomb, so that when the women returned later to what they thought was the correct one, all they found was the empty chamber. It was this vacant crypt, coupled perhaps with a mysterious stranger, that subsequently sparked the notion that Jesus had risen from the dead.

A number of gospel details coincide with this theory. We are told, for instance, that the Sabbath was approaching quickly. This means the sun would have been setting, and Joseph would have been in a hurry. The tomb was a new one (Matt 27:60//Luke 23:53//John 19:41). As opposed to a well-established family vault, this one was probably unmarked. If there were other new tombs in the area, the mistake would have been easy to make. We also know that the earliest of the gospels (Mark) contains no resurrection appearance of Jesus whatsoever. Instead, the story ends at the grave. Furthermore, when the beloved disciple finds Jesus' sepulcher tenantless in the gospel of John, he "saw and believed" (20:8 RSV).

Despite these indicators, the evangelists actively resist the wrong/empty tomb theory. Matthew, Mark, and Luke, for instance, each insist that the women who witnessed Jesus' crucifixion also saw exactly where he was buried (Mark 15:47//Matt 27:61//Luke 23:55). According to Matthew, it is not just any tomb Joseph uses, but his very own (Matt 27:60). Furthermore, when Peter visits the tomb, he does not find the chamber completely void. Instead, Jesus' burial cloths are lying there (Luke 24:13//John 20:5–7). Evidently, they have found the right place.

More important than the location is the effect. According to
Mark, Luke, and John, the empty tomb is *not* sufficient to engender
the faith of the disciples. In Mark, of course, the women depart in
fear and fail to even transmit the message. In Luke, the empty tomb
merely baffles Peter (Luke 24:13). As for John, the object of the disciple's belief is patently *not* Jesus' resurrection. This is made clear by
the context: "and he saw and believed; *for as yet they did not know the
scripture, that [Jesus] must rise from the dead*" (John 20:8–9 RSV, emphasis added). What, then, did the vault convince the disciples of?
Only that Mary was right—someone *had* taken Jesus' body away
(20:2). Thus, the evangelists confirm that the tomb was the right
one; its vacancy, however, was not enough to generate faith in Jesus'
resurrection.

Disciples' Theft

Another popular alternative is that the disciples stole Jesus'
body. They certainly had the means. Joseph of Arimathea is referred
to as a "disciple of Jesus" by both Matthew (Matt 27:57) and John
(John 19:38). The corpse was last in his possession. They also had
the motive. By order of the Jewish and Roman authorities, their beloved Rabbi had been publicly ridiculed and brutally executed.
What better way to retaliate? The disciples could have stolen the
dead body, hidden it away, and then claimed Jesus' victory over
death. Such a victory, of course, would have been tantamount to a
victory over the authorities.

It is Matthew who engages this theory most directly. According
to him, the Jews and Romans took counteractive measures in order
to prevent this very thing from happening:

> The chief priests and the Pharisees gathered before Pilate and said,
> "Sir, we remember how that impostor said, while he was still alive, 'Af-
> ter three days I will rise again.' Therefore order the sepulchre to be
> made secure until the third day, lest his disciples go and steal him
> away, and tell the people, 'He has risen from the dead,' and the last
> fraud will be worse than the first." Pilate said to them, "You have a
> guard of soldiers; go, make it as secure as you can." So they went and
> made the sepulchre secure by sealing the stone and setting a guard.
> (Matt 27:62–66 RSV)

As Matthew's narrative reports, the guards witnessed the angel's dramatic announcement to the women at the tomb. After the women departed, some of the soldiers

> went into the city and told the chief priests all that had taken place. And when they had assembled with the elders and taken counsel, they gave a sum of money to the soldiers and said, "Tell people, 'His disciples came by night and stole him away while we were asleep.' And if this comes to the governor's ears, we will satisfy him and keep you out of trouble." So they took the money and did as they were directed; and this story has been spread among the Jews to this day. (Matt 28:11–15 RSV)

If Matthew's testimony is correct, this "conspiracy theory" is as old as the resurrection story. Matthew suggests that the rumor originated with the chief priests. But while this evangelist endeavors to explain why it would have been impossible for the disciples to steal Jesus' body, his credibility immediately comes into question. Not only is Matthew the only evangelist to depict guards at Jesus' burial place, he is also connected to the disciples! If they perpetrated the hoax, and the gospels were written by them or their close associates, then their "reports" may be no more than propaganda aimed at promulgating their deception and discrediting the authorities.

As far as this theory is concerned, then, the gospels themselves become inadmissible as evidence against it. If we rule them out along with the other writings from the early Christians, we are left with virtually no "objective" documentation to substantiate Jesus' resurrection. In other words, the only ones who claim to have seen the risen Jesus are his followers!

On the face of it, this explanation is convincing. However, at least four objections may be leveled against it. First, while it is true that only Jesus' followers wrote of his resurrection, one of them was not a disciple at the time of his encounter. Just the opposite. Saul of Tarsus was a persecutor of Christians when Jesus purportedly appeared to him. It was on the basis of this experience that Saul underwent a radical conversion and became the Apostle Paul, the most prolific of the NT authors. Prior to his conversion, then, Saul of Tarsus constitutes what would arguably be the ideal objective witness.

A second difficulty with this theory lies in the sheer number of gospels and the disagreements among them concerning Jesus' resurrection. All of this makes for poor propaganda. If the disciples had truly conspired together in order to exact revenge, we would expect to see more harmony—especially among their written documents! In other words, if they were trying to cover up the truth, why would they sabotage their own credibility by publishing conflicting accounts? It would have been far more prudent to simply stick to one story.

A third objection pertains to the element of doubt that is common to these reports. If the gospels were created solely to promote the fallacy that Jesus rose, when in fact his corpse was sequestered away somewhere, we would expect to see the disciples portrayed as absolutely certain of this event. Yet they are not. The evangelists readily acknowledge that even Jesus' closest followers struggled to accept his resurrection. In Mark, the women fail to respond appropriately to the news at the tomb. Matthew and Luke both report disbelief among the disciples (Matt 28:17; Luke 24:41). Only in John's gospel does this mistrust serve a rhetorical purpose. John manages to use Thomas's initial refusal to accept the testimony of his companions as a way to encourage his readers to believe in the absence of empirical proof:

> Jesus said to him, "Have you come to believe because you have seen me? Blessed are those who have not seen and have believed." (John 20:29 NAB)

Such rhetoric, however, plays no part in the doubts described by the other evangelists. If they were really trying to advance a scam, why would they deliberately interject suspicion into their own claim?

A final objection to this theory appeals to events that transpired after those recorded in the gospels. Tradition claims that the disciples and their associates subsequently traveled throughout the empire spreading the "good news" and establishing communities of believers. According to various legends, all of these men faced persecution and eventually died martyr's deaths. Peter, Andrew, and Philip were crucified. Bartholomew was flayed and beheaded. Simon was sawed in two. James the Greater died by the sword, James the Less by the club, Matthew and Thomas by the spear, and Jude and Matthias by the halberd. Only John died a "natural" death, following years of exile on the island of Patmos.

Historically, of course, some of these legends are easier to substantiate than others. Nevertheless, it is certain that some, if not all, of Jesus' earliest followers were willing to die for their beliefs. That they were *not* goaded into death by the charisma of their leader is clear. The gospels agree that the disciples immediately deserted Jesus at his arrest. By contrast, they died insisting that Jesus had risen from the dead. It was this event that supposedly transformed and emboldened them. But if the resurrection was only a scheme to get back at the authorities, then their willingness to die becomes difficult to explain. In effect, they would have died for a hoax.

While the martyrdom of the disciples is strong evidence in favor of their innocence, it is not ironclad. Our recent history is replete with examples of zealous individuals willing to sacrifice their lives "for the cause." Consider the World War II Japanese kamikaze pilots, the Waco Branch Davidians, the al-Qaeda hijackers of September 11, and the Palestinian suicide bombers. In each case, a profound and desperate hatred of a governing power, coupled with the promise of eternal reward, led to the ultimate act of forfeiture. Was this the mindset of Jesus' disciples?

If it is, the gospels should reflect strong anti-establishment sentiments. But they don't. At least, not in the way that one might expect. That all four of the gospels staunchly oppose the *Jewish* leadership is obvious. And indeed, a few of the very first Christians died at the hands of the Jews. But if the gospels were written between 70 and 90 CE as the vast majority of scholars contend, then the authority of the Jews would have already been usurped by the Romans following the assault on Jerusalem in 70 CE. Assuming the gospels functioned as instruments of propaganda (as this theory suggests), such a rigorous campaign against a power that had already been deposed makes little sense.

If anything, the *Roman* authorities posed a far greater threat to the early Christians. Not only did they crucify Jesus, they were also responsible for most of the atrocities against his followers. Consider, for instance, the report of the Roman historian Tacitus (55–117 CE) concerning their suffering under Emperor Nero (54–68 CE):

> Nero fastened the guilt and inflicted the most exquisite tortures on a class hated for their abominations, called Christians by the populace. . . . Accordingly, an immense multitude was convicted . . . of hatred against mankind. Mockery of every sort was added to their deaths. Covered with the skins of beasts, they were torn to death by dogs, or nailed to crosses, or set fire to, and when daylight had expired, they served as nocturnal lights. (*Ann.* 15.44)

In fact, it was the severity of these persecutions and similar ones under Emperor Domitian (81–96 CE) that inspired the dreadful apocalyptic judgment envisioned in the book of Revelation.

The evangelists, however, go out of their way to exonerate Rome from its involvement in Jesus' death. In Mark, for instance, Pilate never declares Jesus guilty. Rather, he offers to release Jesus to the crowd, which elects Barabbas instead. When those assembled insist that Pilate crucify Jesus, the governor asks, "Why, what evil has he done?" (Mark 15:14 RSV). Eventually Pilate capitulates, but only to satisfy the masses (Mark 15:1–15).

Matthew, Luke, and John defend Pilate even more emphatically. Matthew literally has Pilate washing his hands of Jesus' blood as the Jews accept total responsibility for it (Matt 27:24–25). In both Luke and John, Pilate explicitly declares Jesus innocent three times (Luke 23:3, 14, 22; John 18:38; 19:4, 6). Luke even goes so far as to attribute to Herod's soldiers the mockery and scourging Jesus presumably suffered under the Roman guards (Luke 23:11).

Clearly, these portrayals serve an apologetic purpose. The evangelists were attempting to make Christianity as agreeable to the Roman Empire as possible, despite Rome's role in Jesus' demise. This evidence suggests that the early Christians sought to coexist peacefully in the empire and to avoid persecution wherever possible. Hardly the behavior of anti-establishment zealots!

It is difficult, therefore, to square the contents of the gospels with the theory that the disciples stole Jesus' body. In the absence of any antagonism toward their primary persecutors, the martyrdom of the disciples must have been predicated upon something else. Having formerly abandoned Jesus, something must have happened to them between Gethsemane and Pentecost to cause such a dramatic transformation—something more compelling than either an empty tomb or a concealed cadaver.

An Apparition

Some have proposed that the disciples merely *thought* that they saw the risen Jesus, and that this is what subsequently encouraged them. Perhaps it was a hallucination, a ghost, or some other psychologically induced vision. The disciples had, after all, experienced considerable trauma. Judas' nighttime ambush had caught them completely off guard. They probably felt ashamed for having abandoned Jesus, and they must have been heartbroken by the ignominy of his death. Understandably, they were also scared. Judas would have known where they had gathered. If he had betrayed Jesus, they could presume to be next. No doubt they were terrified, exhausted, depressed, and bewildered. When the report of the empty tomb came back, perhaps it was enough to trigger some sort of delusion. Like frightened children in a haunted house, maybe their imaginations took over, and they saw something that they took to be Jesus' specter.

Again, various facets of the gospels may contribute to this theory. Fear is a dominant theme in three of these accounts. Trembling and astonishment overcome Mark's women at the tomb (Mark 16:8). In Luke, the disciples are initially "startled and frightened" by Jesus (Luke 24:36). In John, the eleven timidly locked themselves in a room just prior to their encounter (John 20:19). That Jesus was only an apparition is further suggested by his mysterious ability to suddenly appear in a secured place (Luke 24:36; John 20:19, 26) or to vanish before their eyes (Luke 24:31). Perhaps prompted by Jesus' earlier predictions that he would conquer death, the disciples imagined what they subconsciously desired to see.

It is almost certain that this possibility had already occurred to the evangelists. In particular, both Luke and John discount it by underscoring the physical nature of Jesus' resurrection:

> As they were saying this, Jesus himself stood among them. But they were startled and frightened, and supposed that they saw a spirit. And he said to them, "Why are you troubled, and why do questionings rise in your hearts? See my hands and my feet, that it is I myself; handle me, and see; for a spirit has not flesh and bones as you see that I have. And while they still disbelieved for joy and wondered, he said to them, "Have you anything here to eat?" They gave him a piece of broiled fish, and he took it and ate before them. (Luke 24:36–43 RSV)

> But [Thomas] said to [the disciples], "Unless I see in his hands the print of the nails, and place my finger in the mark of the nails, and place my hand in his side, I will not believe." Eight days later . . . [Jesus] said to Thomas, "Put your finger here, and see my hands; and put out your hand, and place it in my side; do not be faithless, but believing." (John 20:25–27 RSV)

According to these evangelists, then, the risen Jesus was decidedly *not* some sort of phantom. The disciples encountered him tangibly.

Botched Execution

The corporeal character of Jesus' resurrection leads to a final theory. Some have suggested that Jesus never really died on the cross. Rather, he was presumed to be dead and taken down prematurely. Unconscious at first, perhaps he came to in the tomb and stumbled out unnoticed either before the rock was rolled into place or after it was removed. He would have had a couple of days to regain his strength before appearing to his disciples. He may not even have intended to "trick" them; perhaps he himself believed that he had risen. His reunion with them certainly would have been persuasive. Having witnessed him alive, the disciples would now be willing to go forth, spread his teachings, and, if necessary, even die for what they saw.

The fact that Jesus still has his wounds and is able to eat and drink with his disciples lends credence to this theory. But is there any indication that Jesus was taken off the cross prematurely? According to the gospel of John, both of the men crucified next to Jesus are still alive when their legs are broken. Jesus is supposed dead at this point, so his legs are spared (John 19:32–33). Jesus' relatively early expiration is noted in Mark's gospel as well. When Joseph requests Jesus' body, Pilate "wonders"—a word Mark usually uses to connote astonishment—if Jesus had indeed already died. He thus summons a centurion to confirm it (Mark 15:44). This evidence suggests Jesus' time on the cross may not have been sufficient to kill him.

A host of circumstantial details can be leveled against this theory. Jesus' scourging would have sapped his strength and endurance (Mark 15:15; Matt 27:26; Luke 23:16; John 18:1). Presumably, this is why Simon had to carry his cross (Mark 15:21; Matt 27:32; Luke 23:26). Then there is the assessment of the Roman guards (Mark 15:39, 45; John 19:33) and the piercing of Jesus' side (John 19:34). There are the soldiers (Matt 27:62–66), the stone (Mark 15:46; Matt 27:60), and the angels (Mark 16:5; Matt 28:2; Luke 24:4; John 20:12) at the tomb. We also have Jesus' instantaneous appearances (Luke 24:36; John 20:19, 26) and disappearances (Luke 24:31). Individually, these details are not insurmountable. Collectively, however, they become difficult to account for in proving this theory.

There are two other considerations that bear upon this proposal. First, both Luke and John indicate that the disciples had a difficult time recognizing Jesus. It would be reasonable to attribute some of this to the element of surprise—they simply wouldn't have expected to see him again. This is evidently the case with Mary Magdalene when she mistakes Jesus for the gardener at the tomb in John 20:15. But according to the evangelists, this is not simply a problem experienced initially. In Luke, Jesus accompanies two disciples as many as seven miles and shares a meal with them before they catch on that it is he (Luke 24:13–31). In John, even after the disciples recognize Jesus on the shore and eat breakfast with him, there still seems to be a question about his identity (John 21:12). These accounts suggest that while Jesus has retained certain physical characteristics, such as his wounds, there is something qualitatively different about his appearance.

Perhaps the strongest argument against a bungled crucifixion emerges only once it is followed to its logical conclusion. If Jesus did not die on the cross, he would have died eventually. Moreover, his death would have furnished a corpse. Had the disciples known about his eventual death, they inevitably would have figured out what had transpired, and their missionary zeal would have subsided. Had the Jews or Romans known about it, they surely would have exploited it. There can be no more effective way—then or now—to bring Christianity to an end than by producing Jesus' remains. But they never surfaced.

So what became of Jesus' body? Only Luke endeavors to answer this question. The conclusion to his gospel states that on Easter evening, Jesus

> led [his disciples] out as far as Bethany, and lifting up his hands he blessed them. While he blessed them, he parted from them, and was carried up into heaven. (Luke 24:50–51 RSV)

This account of Jesus' ascension conflicts slightly with Luke's portrayal of the same event at the beginning of Acts. There, Jesus "presented himself alive after his passion . . . during forty days" (Acts 1:3 RSV). Following this period, Jesus brought his disciples out to the Mount of Olives, and as they were looking on, he was lifted up, and a cloud took him out of their sight. (Acts 1:9 RSV)

The variations in timing and location suggest that Luke may have received his information from more than one source. Thus, although Luke is the only evangelist to write of Jesus' ascension, the event itself appears to have been corroborated by at least two independent traditions. At any rate, it effectively answers the question about Jesus' body. We must conclude, therefore, that while some aspects of the resurrection accounts may be explained by this theory, the gospels ultimately resist the notion that Jesus somehow survived the cross.

Conclusion

Having considered the most common explanations of Jesus' resurrection in light of the evidence from the gospels, we are now in a position to summarize our results. The incredulous nature of this event automatically lends itself to skepticism. And while some facets of these accounts may provoke suspicion, others are specifically cited to counter it. The evangelists obviously anticipated the objections of their readers and considered the alternatives. The question is, did they fabricate their stories in order to make the resurrection more plausible, or were their reports historically grounded—at least to the best of their knowledge? We simply cannot answer this question with absolute certainty.

The documented courage of the earliest Christians, however, suggests that they experienced something transformational long before these gospels were written. Ostensibly, then, it is this event that engendered the gospels, and not the gospels that engendered this event. According to these writings, the incident in question was *not* an empty tomb, a stolen body, an apparition, or a botched execution. Indeed, if the resurrection were so easy to dismiss, one wonders whether Christianity could have survived for two thousand years. Yet this faith, and the gospels that bear witness to it, both continue to endure, and they do so largely on the basis of this single, extraordinary premise.

Endnotes

FROM JAMES CAMERON TO JESUS CHRIST

1. James Cameron, acceptance speech for Oscar for Best Director of *Titanic, The 70th Annual Academy Awards,* ABC, March 23, 1998.

2. Special Feature Oscars, "I'm King of the World: 'Titanic' Ties with 'Ben Hur' for 11 Oscars," CNN, March 23, 1998, http://www.cnn.com/SPECIALS/1998/showbiz/oscars/news/main.oscars.write/(accessed April 17, 2004).

3. Editorial, "Oops," *Oregonian* (Portland, Ore.), sec. B, Mar 27, 2001, http://www.oregonlive.com/search/oregonian/ (accessed April 17, 2004).

4. Tom Shales, "A Show of Shows," *Washington Post,* sec. D, March 24, 1998, http://pqasb.pqarchiver.com/washingtonpost/27716389.html?did=27716389&FMT=ABS&FMTS=FT&date=Mar+24C+1998&author=Tom+Shales&desc=A+Show+of+ShowsA+Hollywood+Does+Itself+Proud (accessed April 17, 2004).

5. Liz Smith, "Why Leo Skipped It," *Newsday* (Long Island, N.Y.), sec. A, March 25, 1998, http://pqasb.pqarchiver.com/newsday/27763361.html?did=27763361&FMT=ABS&FMTS=FT&date=Mar+25C+1998&author=Liz+Smith&desc=Why+Leo+Skipped+It (accessed April 17, 2004).

6. Marylynn Uricchio, "When the Ceremony's Over, the Celebrities Party All Night," *Pittsburgh Post-Gazette* (Pittsburgh, Pa.), sec. F, March 25, 1998, http://www.post-gazette.com/magazine/19980325boscars1.asp (accessed May 18, 2004).

7. Editorial, "Familiar Pains on Oscar Night," *New York Times,* sec. A, March 25, 1998, http://query.nytimes.com/gst/abstract.html?res=FA0813FF355C0C768EDDAA0894D0494D81 (accessed April 17, 2004).

8. William Lane, *The Gospel of Mark: The English Text with Introduction, Exposition, and Notes* (New International Commentary on the New Testament; Grand Rapids, Mich.: Eerdmans, 1974), 573.

9. Wilfrid J. Harrington, *Mark* (New Testament Message 4; Wilmington, Del.: Michael Glazier, 1979), 240.

10. Ched Myers, *Binding the Strong Man: A Political Reading of Mark's Story of Jesus* (Maryknoll, N.Y.: Orbis, 1988), 389.

1—JESUS' GENEALOGY

1. Josephus, *Ant.* 5.330.
2. For instance, *Midr.* Gen 23:1 lists Bathsheba, Ruth, and Rahab among twenty-two "women of valor." As for Tamar, her virtues are extolled by the first-century Jewish philosopher Philo of Alexandria (*Virt.* 221).

4—MINISTERIAL FRAMEWORKS

1. Conceptually adapted from Werner H. Kelber, *Mark's Story of Jesus* (Philadelphia: Fortress, 1979).

10—JESUS' RESURRECTION

1. Paranormal Phenomena, "The Houdini Séance," About.com, http: // paranormal.about.com/library/weekly/aa103000a.htm (accessed April 17, 2004).

Recommended References

GOSPEL COMMENTARIES

Bock, Darrell L. *Luke*. Baker Exegetical Commentary on the New Testament 3A–B. 2 vols.. Grand Rapids, Mich.: Baker, 1994.

Brown, Raymond E. *The Gospel According to John*. Anchor Bible 29–29A; 2 vols. New York: Doubleday, 1994.

Davies, W. D., and Dale C. Allison. *A Critical and Exegetical Commentary on the Gospel According to Saint Matthew*. International Critical Commentary. 3 vols. Edinburgh: T&T Clark, 1988–1997.

Evans, Craig A. *Mark 8:27–16:20*. Word Biblical Commentary 34B. Nashville: Thomas Nelson, 2001.

Fitzmyer, Joseph A. *The Gospel According to Luke*. Anchor Bible 28–28A. 2 vols. New York: Doubleday, 1981–1985.

France, R. T. *The Gospel of Mark: A Commentary on the Greek Text*. The New International Greek Testament Commentary 2. Grand Rapids: Eerdmans, 2002.

Guelich, Robert A. *Mark 1–8:26*. Word Biblical Commentary 34A. Dallas: Word Books, 1989.

Marcus, Joel. *Mark 1–8: A New Translation with Introduction and Commentary*. Anchor Bible 27. New York: Doubleday, 2000.

Marshall, I. H. *The Gospel of Luke: A Commentary on the Greek Text*. The New International Greek Testament Commentary 3. Grand Rapids: Eerdmans, 1978.

Moloney, Francis. *The Gospel of Mark: A Commentary*. Peabody, Mass.: Hendrickson, 2002.

Nolland, John. *The Gospel of Luke*. Word Biblical Commentary 35A–C. 3 vols. Dallas: Word Books, 1990–1994.

SPECIFIC STUDIES

Bridge, Steven L. *"Where the Eagles Are Gathered": The Deliverance of the Elect in Lukan Eschatology.* Journal for the Study of the New Testament Supplement Series 240. Sheffield: Sheffield Academic Press, 2003.

Brown, Raymond E. *The Birth of the Messiah: A Commentary on the Infancy Narratives in Matthew and Luke, updated and revised.* Anchor Bible Reference Library. New York: Doubleday, 1993.

_____. *The Death of the Messiah: From Gethsemane to the Grave: A Commentary on the Passion Narratives in the Four Gospels.* Anchor Bible Reference Library. 2 vols. New York: Doubleday, 1994.

Index of Ancient Sources

Index of Subjects